GARDENS OF SCOTLAND 2006

Contents

FRONT COVER
by Steve Carroll, Illustrator

Printed by Inglis Allen, 40 Townsend Place, Kirkcaldy, Fife.

Chairman's Message

It was with the greatest of pleasure that we received the good news last summer that HRH The Duchess of Rothesay had graciously agreed to honour us by becoming our President for five years and we very much hope that we will be able to welcome her before too long to one of the many gardens which so kindly opens for us. I find it hard to believe that 2006 is my last year as Chairman but feel most fortunate to be in situ for our 75th Birthday. Juliet Edmonstone has written a short history of Scotland's Gardens Scheme, which you will find elsewhere in the handbook and I hope, will enjoy reading. The Queens Nursing Institute Scotland have launched a competition for hospitals, hospices and residential homes in Scotland, to make a garden or improve an existing one, entitled "Gardening for Health" which is most appropriate for C21, when we rely so heavily on cars and computers. We are carrying this theme on to "Gardening Scotland" the first weekend in June when we celebrate with Dobbies (who will be almost twice our age at 140) when we share their stand at Ingliston.

2006 seems to be the year for special birthday's as the National Trust for Scotland are 75 and Perennial (GRBS) 50 so please help them and our other beneficiaries by visiting as many of our wonderful gardens as you can.

Charlotte Hunt

SCOTLAND'S GARDENS SCHEME

A registered Scottish charity founded in 1931 to support the Queen's Nursing Institute Scotland - see page 9.

Over 350 gardens of all sizes open to the public on one or more days each year.

Garden owners donate entry fees and revenue from teas and plant sales to support our beneficiaries.

The Gardens Fund of the National Trust for Scotland became our second principal beneficiary in 1952 - see page 10.

We also support Perennial (GRBS) and the Royal Gardeners' Orphan Fund - see page 12.

In 2004 149 registered charities of the owners' choice received up to 40% of the day's takings;

145 volunteers work in 27 Districts throughout Scotland to help the Scheme.

In 2005 £188,837 was distributed to charities.

CARING AND SHARING
Roots and reminiscences of Scotland's Gardens Scheme
By
Juliet Edmonstone

75 years ago our wonderful SGS was born. A well-rooted hardy perennial if ever there was one and, like so many success stories, the right idea at the right time, for the right people. Instant popularity was ensured by this brilliant combination of horticulture and an enjoyable opportunity to admire the neighbour's garden whilst supporting the much loved District Nurses. Following the example of HM King George V who immediately opened Balmoral gardens twice weekly, private owners threw open their gates too, responding enthusiastically to this new idea of sharing their gardens with appreciative visitors, all contributing to so worthy a cause!

It all began in 1931 following the success of the National Gardens Scheme. With the warm support of HRH The Duchess of York (later Queen Elizabeth, the Queen Mother), Violet, Countess of Mar and Kellie (Chairman of the Scottish Queen's Institute of District Nursing) gathered together the first SGS committee under the chairmanship of the Countess of Minto. Under her a network of County Organisers were appointed who, though guided from above, ran their own area according to its needs - just as it is today. Much credit is due to the energy and personal commitment of these ladies and their successors who happily persuaded garden owners to open and ensured that the Scheme ran smoothly. Lady Rosebery, for instance, rescued a last minute crisis by selling 2,000 daffodils in the streets of Edinburgh – a really most unusual sight for those days!

Most of those early gardens belonged to what one might call smart county families and opened on any day of the week - reflecting perhaps that the privileged and more leisured life-style afforded by these beautiful properties also brought with it a deep and traditional sense of public service. The example and goodwill of that generation lives on in the thousands of equally dedicated and public-spirited owners who support us today and in a much more hands-on way than in the past! Nowadays the Scheme welcomes some 350 gardens of every type imaginable and valuable income also comes from dedicated National Trust for Scotland days, contributions from 'ever-open gardens', busy plant sales, and popular village openings.

The first yellow handbook of 1932 listed over 500 gardens in return for a 'voluntary contribution, and was really a simplified version of today's. This surprisingly remained until 1962 when a charge of 1/- was made but the garden openings had dropped to 238. In 1971 the handbook burst into colour for 20p and became a forerunner of our present one.

Originally the idea was that the Scheme should contribute to the training and pensions of the Queen's nurses, but with the introduction of the NHS by Aneurin Bevan in 1948 their training became the responsibility of the Government. It was still essential, however, to contribute to pension funds of £1 a week for the 300 nurses who had not worked the requisite 15 years before retiring in order to become eligible and also to help those in 'necessitous circumstances'. There was, in addition, the nurses' holiday home Colinton Cottage, the Christmas Gift Fund and also projects outwith NHS funding.

The Queen's Institute of District Nursing grew out of the visionary efforts of William Rathbone, a Liverpool businessman. Concerned at the total lack of nursing care for the poor, he paid his wife's nurse –a Mrs Robinson – and another nurse to go out into the community where conditions of terrible deprivation had resulted from insufficient planning during the vast expansion of cities in the Industrial Revolution. There were, it seems, plenty of industrial entrepreneurs in those days but very few people with a social conscience. He then enlisted the help of Florence Nightingale and in 1862, established a nurses training school attached to Liverpool Royal Infirmary.

In 1887 Queen Victoria allocated £70,000 from her Jubilee gift from the ladies of Great Britain towards 'Improved means of nursing for the sick poor' and two years later the first of many Training Centres was set up in Edinburgh where nurses spent six months learning all the additional skills they would require out in the community. These ranged from budgeting to home hygiene, tuberculosis to cookery and were learned in order 'to understand the difficulties and outlook of those with whom they would come into such intimate contact'. By 1927 every village in the country had its own Nurse and 65 years after William Rathbone's inspirational lead district nursing became an integral part of British life!

To understand these remarkable women, I can do no better than to quote from Isobel, Marchioness of Graham, the first General Organiser, whose eloquent reports and first-hand memories paint such a vivid picture of life not all that long ago. 'Such were the standards, the understanding and the care given by a Queen's Nurse', Lady Graham wrote, 'that she could penetrate districts - in her navy blue uniform with its Queen's badge and her little black bag of equipment - that no policeman could go alone'. They paid a high price for their devotion to the communities they served. 'Long hours on call night and day, arduous treks by bicycle round back streets, up steep tenement stairs, across bleak moors and stormy seas in all weathers'

As they put their knowledge and skill at the service of the sick, Queen's nurses became the trusted friend and confidante of their patients - chatting away as they washed them, made beds and aired the rooms. They were without doubt both saint and hero as we see only too vividly from a report sent back – probably around the turn of the century - by one of the early nurses to the Outer Hebrides. On her first confinement visit she is rowed to one of the islands and arrives drenched in sea water to find her landlady's dwelling is a typical two apartment with mud floors. One room, she notes with horror is where they all sleep 'regardless of age and sex' and explains that this would make her ill! There are no cupboards or drawers and the second room has only a kitchen fire in the middle and a smoke hole in the roof. There is little to cook anyway save mutton, herring, eggs, onion and potatoes. Even worse, there is virtually no fruit or even milk with which to make porridge. Her Christmas dinner is salt herring and baked sago and, not surprisingly, she is miserable and homesick, not helped by the fact that of course her patients only speak Gaelic! Despite it all, and with nobody to talk to, she writes, 'I am happy in my work and my patients try to be kind to me. Poor souls, they have so little interest and nothing to be seen but water and hills'.

Another writes from a mining district that although she 'has come to the last place on earth, it would be a real wrench to part from my people whose faces light up with welcome when one goes in and whose dull, hard lot one does brighten'. She speaks heart-warmingly of 16 year old Janet struggling to look after 5 younger siblings after their mother's death.

Far from being brought to a standstill by the war, the infant SGS flourished although garden openings understandably dropped from 500 to 300 as gardeners left for the war and some gardens were damaged and even destroyed by bombing. Proceeds, however, actually increased as, in true British spirit, garden owners tried to ignore the weeds and dug for victory by growing vegetables (for sale of course!) in the flower beds. Tea was patriotically served on the lawns… without sugar. Such was the esteem in which garden openings were held that extra petrol was allowed for special buses to bring visitors from the mines and factories (others came by bicycle, pram and even bath chair!) and owners were issued with special application forms for sufficient petrol to mow the lawn - once a month!

In 1942 Lady Graham's garden was opened with a rousing speech by the Duchess of Roxburgh in which she spoke of the 'comfort it was to the men and women of the forces to know that in times of trouble and sickness, the District Nurse was on call at all times of the day and night to the homes they had had to leave behind', and a grateful visitor replied 'I have enjoyed and seen more things this afternoon than anything in money could possibly repay'. I don't think you can earn more praise than that, except possibly from the harassed official at Dundee bus station who, when asked for the Glamis queue, replied 'Lady it's not a queue, it's an evacuation!' In those days cakes were often provided by local bakeries and great was the excitement when ice-cream became legal again! Nowadays the QNIS, with our agreement, disburses the SGS funds to selected Scottish Community Nursing projects which help to raise standards of patient care, such as the development of Best Practice Statements and a CD Rom on Dementia for use by Community Nursing staff.

In 1952 and after much discussion on the merits of 'rival suitors', it was decided to appoint the Gardens Fund of the National Trust for Scotland (founded the same year as SGS mainly due to the inspiration of Sir John Stirling Maxwell of Pollock) as a second beneficiary. The Trust was then chaired by the present Lord Wemyss, an elder statesman of the heritage world whose intelligence and wit has long charmed every generation. Our relationship with the Trust has remained a most happy and successful one - their first disbursement for nearly £2,000 has now grown to around £50,000 every year.

Garden staff at Haddo House 1886   (photograph courtesy of The National Trust for Scotland)

In 1961 an important decision was taken to allow owners – if they chose - to allocate 40% of their gross takings (average £60) to a registered charity of their own choice. Altogether 170 different charities a year benefitted from this unique and popular arrangement. At the same time it was agreed to make small annual disbursements to the Royal Gardeners Benevolent Fund (now Perennial) and The Royal Gardeners Orphan Fund.

That first year the Scheme raised £2,18100 (including donations) and in 1932, which was the first full year, 577 gardens had more than doubled that figure to £5,400 - the equivalent today of £242,800. Records show that each decade after that more or less doubled the proceeds and during the 1980s annual income more than trebled to an incredible £178,700! The average return from each garden then was £250, which would be £493 today. By 2000 annual proceeds had leapt to £266,800 and in 2005 garden owners raised over £300,000 for the first time. Their choice of charities is an interesting reflection of modern thinking, ranging from the local village church to medical and cancer related charities, hospices and the many very personal choices of the owners. In 1982 SGS won the British Tourist Authority award for 'Outstanding contribution to tourism' and thus was recognised handsomely the contribution the Scheme makes to Scotland and its way of life.

SGS is lucky to have been organised and chaired by some very special personalities and I am most grateful to Sir Ilay Campbell of Succoth (our Vice-President) for his reminiscences of them during his many years of wise counsel on the Executive Committees of the National Trust for Scotland and ourselves. Lady Graham served as General Organiser for 23 years until 1953. 'She was' remembers Sir Ilay 'an outstanding organiser who served four successive Chairmen and guided the boat through the choppy seas of the war years'. She also compiled meticulous lists of the takings from each garden and county which were circulated and publicised, possibly to encourage the merest - and most ladylike - hint of competition! Later, as County Organiser for Stirling, she became my friend and mentor who modestly hid her intelligence and efficiency. She was succeeded by Alice Maconochie who served for 19 years 'Alice's special brand of slightly caustic humour' says Sir Ilay 'will be recalled by all who worked with her – and none worked harder than she. All Scotland knew her and she knew all Scotland – rather too well for its liking!'

Poppy Davenport, who served for 11 years and started the Garden Tours, will be 'best remembered for her efficiency and humour and Mrs Moffat 'for her smiling face and impeccable dress sense!' Since 1982, Robin St.Clair Ford has been our Director and his conscientious and fruitful commitment to the modernisation and image of the Scheme has achieved record results. His Garden Tours are conducted with customary cheerfulness!

The first Chairman, Marian, Countess of Minto was succeeded by The Duchess of Roxburghe and then by the Countess of Haddington before herself serving a second term. Sir Ilay admired greatly her 'exceptional charm and organisational ability'. Mrs Alistair Balfour of Dawyck then took over. She was my first Chairman and her charismatic personality left a lasting impression. Sir Ilay remembers her 'unique blend of elegance and delightful wit.' I remember her consummate skill in conducting a meeting - a lesson to us all. If anyone asked a stupid question, or one which she had no intention of answering, she would fix the offender with a fascinated expression, pause and murmur in a deep voice, honed to perfection by her broadcasting career, 'How....er....interesting. Shall we move on'.

After 14 years she was succeeded by Lady Minto's daughter-in-law, Minnie (also Lady Minto) - a charming and diligent American. Sir Ilay recalls her dedication and enthuiasm 'Everyone was captivated by her fairy-tale princess looks and her honest to goodness niceness'. The Hon. Mrs Macnab of Macnab and I were her vice-chairmen and I shall never forget the dignity with which she conducted herself during her last painful fight against cancer.

Minnie was succeeded by Diana whose energy and natural authority made her an excellent chairman. She was followed by the late Barbara Findlay who, despite serious ill health, devoted a great deal of time not only to the Scheme but also to visiting every garden she could. Barbara's successor, Kirsty Maxwell Stuart, with her practical, friendly nature and knowledge of plants, was an equally popular Chairman and Charlotte Hunt, also an experienced gardener, is now carrying the baton into the 21st century, liaising with other organisations and introducing new ideas with great success.

Together they, the District and County Organisers, Honorary Treasurers and other volunteers - without whose often unsung efforts the Scheme would not exist - have forged the SGS of today. The head office is bursting with technology and our web-site and modernised handbook ensure that the maximum amount of visitors can admire and learn from gardens large and small, traditional and modern. The enduring appeal of sharing and caring for our gardens and our charities is as robust and evergreen as it was 75 years ago!

Copyright JE 2005

THE QUEEN'S NURSING INSTITUTE SCOTLAND
Patron: Her Majesty The Queen

31 Castle Terrace Edinburgh EH1 2EL
Tel 0131 229 2333   Fax 0131 228 9066
Registered Charity SC005751

Founded by Royal Charter in 1889, the Queen's Nursing Institute trained and supervised District Nurses throughout Scotland, until 1970 and assisted in the setting up of District Nursing Associations. Since then it has worked to educate, promote and support Community Nurses in primary care. The Queen's Nursing Institute is a registered charity concerned with the welfare of over 700 Queen's Nurses on the mailing list. The following projects are made possible by the generous donation from Scotland's Gardens Scheme. Each of these projects focuses on current unmet needs within the community.

An evaluation of a community befriending programme for young people with cystic fibrosis and their carers in Lothian
A Befriending Programme for children with Cystic Fibrosis has been developed by a partnership of The Sick Children's Hospital Edinburgh, Queen Margaret University College and The Butterfly Trust. Young people with Cystic Fibrosis have difficulty in meeting as a group due to their susceptibility to cross infection, especially chest infections. The one to one befriending programme aims to overcome the isolation faced by this group through regular contact and support.

Development of local health visitors' health work with the community in the Piershill area of Edinburgh
This project is led by a small group of health visitors in a small, deprived area of Edinburgh with access to a local community health flat, where it is hoped to use a community development approach to improving health and reducing the levels of stress experienced by their clients and families.

Smoking cessation in later life: enhancing the knowledge, attitudes and practice of members of the primary care team who work with older people
An evidence based smoking cessation training package is being developed to enable health professionals to give intervention and support to older people giving up smoking.

Training in motivational interviewing for health professionals working with clients who have mental health problems and/or drug and alcohol related problems
Ten nurses are being funded, over a seven month period, to work with a disadvantaged client group in Edinburgh to learn motivational interviewing skills as an effective model of working with patients and clients with complex health problems.

Welfare of Retired Queen's Nurses
Continuing support and care for retired Queen's Nurses who have given much of their time and effort to the community. Pensions, visiting schemes, special grants, group holidays, newsletters and annual gatherings are offered to retired Queen's Nurses.

Chairman: Sir David Carter MD, FRCS(Ed), FRSE
Nurse Director: Mrs Julia Quickfall, MSc, B.Nurs., SRN., DN., Hv Cert, MIHM
WWW.qnis.org.uk   E-mail: office@qnis.org.uk

The National Trust
for Scotland

A Message to Garden Owners from The National Trust for Scotland

December 2005

Like many organisations, 2005 was not an easy year for the Trust both horticulturally and in terms of visitor numbers. The devastating gales at the beginning of the year caused serious damage to some of our finest specimen trees, particularly in our wooded gardens of the West Coast, and the seasons now seem to be so mixed with the spring flowers blooming ever earlier that gardening is becoming more of a challenge, especially keeping colour in the garden for the visitors throughout the summer.

Our visitor numbers started the year excellently but then we ran into the dreaded G8 Summit. The Trust, in common with the rest of the tourism industry, saw its visitor figures badly hit by the TV coverage at what should have been the peak time of year. The one exception to this general decline was Gardens. According to the statistics produced by VisitScotland, visitor numbers to gardens across the whole of Scotland increased by about 5%, thus confirming what my Gardens Department has always been telling me about the priorities for the Trust! Certainly the fact that you can visit the same garden at different times of the year and enjoy a totally different experience does show how important our gardens are in the rich mix of what Scotland can offer its visitors.

In spite of the vagaries of the weather, the SGS garden owners once again overcame adversity and put on a magnificent display. Certainly the standards set by gardens open under the SGS are extraordinarily high and you do the whole horticultural movement proud. And once again the National Trust for Scotland is hugely grateful for the continued support we receive from the SGS. All these funds are ploughed back into our gardens, but we are particularly keen to use the SGS support for training purposes. We do need to give urgent attention to the worrying dearth of young apprentices who see gardening as a long-term career. The Trust recognises the role it has to play in addressing this problem, and is actively seeking to re-invigorate and expand its training facilities at Threave. In this context, we are delighted to work in partnership with the SGS so that we can ensure the long-term skills needed to keep Scotland's gardens at the forefront.

This year both the Trust and the SGS have their 75th anniversaries. We congratulate the SGS on its magnificent achievements over the decades – the hundreds of owners willing to open their gardens to the public are a vibrant testament to your success. We look forward to sharing our joint celebrations. Scotland has the finest gardens in the world – and many of them are within the pages of this booklet. So go out and enjoy them!

Dr Robin Pellew

Robin Pellew.

Chief Executive

A message from Dobbies, by James Barnes

Founded in 1865 by James Dobbie, the name Dobbies has been synonymous with top quality horticulture for 140 years.

Since its flotation on AIM in 1997, the Scottish based company has gone from strength to strength and has emerged as a leading homes and gardens retailer with eleven stores in Scotland and six in England. Dobbies will continue their rapid expansion with the opening of five new developments in the UK across the next two years.

True to their longstanding reputation for plantmanship, Dobbies offers one of the most extensive ranges of plants and core gardening products, with the added benefit of specialist knowledge and advice for expert and novice gardeners. Their drive for quality and innovation has earned them a number of accolades, most recently achieving Gold at the 2005 Ayr and Gateshead Flower Shows.

With the introduction of farm food halls and an expanding homeware and gift range, the company continues to diversify whilst maintaining a horticultural theme throughout the store, from lavender plants to lavender soaps and from apple trees to fresh local apples and preserves.

As the company continues to develop, Dobbies have gained recognition not only for a quality range and value, but also for their ability to inspire educate and entertain, gaining a reputation as a day out destination. Their roots however firmly remain in Horticulture.

Dobbies are delighted to be supporting Scotland Gardens Scheme and to be able to make a contribution.

James Barnes
Chief Executive

THE
ROYAL GARDENERS'
ORPHAN FUND

THE ROYAL GARDENERS' ORPHAN FUND
Registered Charity No: 248746

Our Fund, which helps the orphaned and needy children of professional horticulturists, has been supporting two orphaned children in Scotland over the past year. These two boys have been receiving regular quarterly allowances since the death of their father in 1992 when they were only toddlers. We know from the boys' mother that the help we gave in the early years made the difference between her staying at home to care for her boys and having to return to work much earlier than she would have wished. The boys are now fourteen and fifteen years of age and have grown into well adjusted adolescents who are achieving well, both at school and in their social lives. Our allowance now means that they can enjoy the same out of school activities as their contemporaries and are not significantly financially disadvantaged by their circumstances.

We have also helped a further eight needy children in Scotland during 2005 with such items as a new bed for an eight year old who suffers from asthma, an activity holiday for a youth who suffers from cerebral palsy, and flooring for the new, purpose built housing association property built for a family of five whose youngest child is severely disabled.

The annual donation we receive from Scotland's Gardens Scheme is very much appreciated in helping to fund our ongoing work in Scotland.

If you would like further information regarding our work please contact our Secretary, Mrs Kate Wallis at 10 Deards Wood, Knebworth, Herts SG3 6PG Tel/Fax: 01438 813939

GENERAL INFORMATION

Maps. The maps show the *approximate* locations of gardens – directions can be found in the garden descriptions or full maps on the web site at *www.gardensofscotland.org*

Houses are not open unless specifically stated; where the house or part of the house is shown, an additional charge is usually made.

Lavatories. Private gardens do not normally have outside lavatories. For security reasons, owners have been advised not to admit visitors into their houses.

Dogs. Unless otherwise stated, dogs are usually admitted, but only if kept on a lead. They are not admitted to houses.

Teas. When teas are available this is indicated in the text. An extra charge is usually made for refreshments.

Professional Photographers. No photographs taken in a garden may be used for sale or reproduction without the prior permission of the garden owner.

&. Denotes gardens suitable for wheelchairs.

❀ Shows gardens opening for the first time or re-opening after many years.

✦ Shows gardens with national collections under the auspices of the NCCPG.

The National Trust for Scotland. Members please note that where a National Trust property has allocated an opening day to Scotland's Gardens Scheme which is one of its own normal opening days, members can gain entry on production of their Trust membership card, although donations to Scotland's Gardens Scheme will be most welcome.

Children. All children must be accompanied by an adult.

SCOTLAND'S GARDENS SCHEME

Charity No. SC011337

We welcome gardens large and small and also groups of gardens. If you would like information on how to open your garden for charity please contact us at the address below.

SCOTLAND'S GARDENS SCHEME,
22 RUTLAND SQUARE, EDINBURGH EH1 2BB
Telephone: 0131 229 1870   Fax: 0131 229 0443
E-mail: *office@sgsgardens.fsnet.co.uk*

NAME & ADDRESS: (Block capitals please)

....

....

....

Postcode...............................   Tel:..

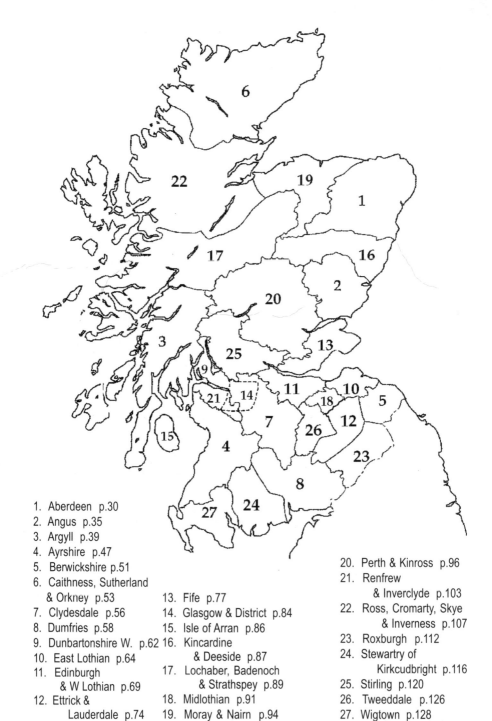

Gardens Open on a Regular Basis or By Appointment

Full details are given in the District List of Gardens

ABERDEEN

23 Don Street, Old Aberdeen	*June - August by appointment*
Blairwood, Aberdeen	*Mid June - beginning October by appointment*
Grandhome, Aberdeen	*By appointment*
Greenridge, Cults	*July & August by appointment*
Gregellen House	*By appointment*
Hatton Castle, Turriff	*By appointment*
Howemill, Craigievar	*By appointment*
Lochan House	*Groups by appointment*
Ploughman's Hall, Old Rayne	*By appointment*

ANGUS

House of Pitmuies, Guthrie, by Forfar	*1 April - 31 October 10am - 5pm*

ARGYLL

26 Kilmartin, Lochgilphead	*1 June - 30 September 10.30am - Dusk*
Achnacloich, Connel	*Daily 8 April - 31 October 10am - 6pm*
An Cala, Ellenabeich	*Daily 1 April - 31 October 10am - 6pm*
Ardchattan Priory, North Connel.	*Daily 1 April - 31 October 9am - 6pm*
Ardkinglas Woodland Garden	*Daily all year round - daylight hours*
Ardmaddy Castle, by Oban	*Daily all year 9am - sunset*
Ardno, Cairndow	*By appointment*
Ascog Hall, Isle of Bute	*Daily (except Mons & Tues)*
	Easter - End Oct 10am - 5pm
Barguillean's "Angus Garden"	*Daily all year 9am - 6pm*
Cnoc-na-Garrie, Ballymeanoch	*April - September or by appointment*
Druimavuic House, Appin	*Daily April, May & June 10am - 6pm*
Druimneil House, Port Appin	*Daily 1 April - 31 October 9am - 6pm*
Eckford, By Dunoon	*Daily 9 April - 6 June 10am - 5pm*
Glecknabae, Isle of Bute	*By appointment Spring - Autumn*
Jura House, Ardfin, Isle of Jura.	*Open all year 9am - 5pm*
Kildalloig, Campbeltown	*By appointment*
Kinlochlaich House Gardens, Appin.	*Open all year 9.30 -5.30 or dusk*
(Except Suns Oct - Mar)	*Suns Apr - Sept 10.30am - 5.30pm*
Torosay Castle Gardens, Isle of Mull	*Gardens open all year*

BERWICKSHIRE
Bughtrig, Leitholm .... 1 June–1 September 11am – 5pm

CAITHNESS, SUTHERLAND & ORKNEY
Kerrachar, Kylesku .... Mid May - mid Sept Tues, Thurs & Suns
.... & By Appt.
Langwell, Berriedale .... By appointment

CLYDESDALE
Baitlaws, Lamington .... By appointment June, July, August
Biggar Park, Biggar .... Groups May - July by appointment

DUNBARTONSHIRE WEST
Glenarn, Rhu .... Daily 21 March - 21 Sept. Sunrise - Sunset

EAST LOTHIAN
Inwood, Carberry .... For details see website www.inwoodgarden.com
.... Groups by appt. Tel: (0131) 665 4550
Shepherd House, Inveresk .... Tues & Thurs 2 - 4pm Apr, May & June
.... & By appointment Tel: 0131 665 2570
Stobshiel House, Humbie .... By appointment Tel: 01875 833646
.... email: wardhersey@aol.com

EDINBURGH & WEST LOTHIAN
61 Fountainhall Road, Edinburgh .... By appointment
Annet House Garden .... Easter -Oct Mon - Sat 10am - 5pm Sun 1 - 4pm
Kirknewton House, Kirknewton .... By appointment Monday - Friday
Newliston, Kirkliston .... Wed - Suns inc. 3 May - 4 June 2 - 6pm

FIFE
Cambo House, Kingsbarns .... Open all year 10am - dusk
Strathtyrum, St Andrews .... Weekdays 1st week of June, August &
.... September 2 - 4.30pm
Wemyss Castle, East Wemyss .... Open Thursday's mid April to end August
.... 12.30 - 6pm

GLASGOW
Invermay, Cambuslang .... April - September by appointment

LOCHABER, BADENOCH & STRATHSPEY
Ardtornish, Lochaline, Morvern .... Open 1 April - 31 October 10am - 6pm

MIDLOTHIAN
The Old Sun Inn, Newhall .... By appointment (most days) 1 May - 30 July

MORAY & NAIRN
Knocknagore, Knockando .... By appointment

PERTH & KINROSS
Ardvorlich, Lochearnhead............................ 7 May to 4 June All day
Bolfracks, Aberfeldy .... 1 April - 31October 10am - 6pm
Braco Castle, Braco .... 1 Apr - Mid Aug 10am - 5pm (Oct Wed - Sun)
.... Other times by appointment.
Cluniemore, Pitlochry................................. 1 May - 1 Oct by appointment
Cluny House, Aberfeldy .... 1 March - 31 October 10am - 6pm
Rossie House, Forgandenny .... 1 March - 31 October by appointment
Scone Palace, Perth .... 1 April - 31 October 9.30 - 5.30pm

RENFREW & INVERCLYDE
Sma'shot Heritage Centre, Paisley................. Weds & Sats 14 June - 15 July 12 noon - 4pm

ROSS, CROMARTY, SKYE & INVERNESS
Abriachan, Loch Ness Side........................... February - November 9am - dusk
An Acarsaid, Ord, Sleat, Isle of Skye .... April - October 10am - 5.30pm
Attadale, Strathcarron .... 1 Apr - end Oct Closed Suns10am - 5.30pm
Balmeanach House, Struan .... Weds & Sats end Apr - mid Oct 11am - 4.30pm
Coiltie Garden, Divach, Drumnadrochit....... 17 June - 23 July Noon - 7pm
.... and by appointment.
Dunvegan Castle, Isle of Skye...................... 21 March - 31 October 10am - 5.30pm
Leathad Ard, Isle of Lewis .... Tues, Thurs, Sats 10 June - 26 August 2 - 6pm
Leckmelm Shrubbery & Arboretum .... 1 April - 31 October 10am - 6pm
The Hydroponicum, Achiltibuie .... 3 Apr - 30 Sep & Mon - Fri in Oct

ROXBURGH
Floors Castle, Kelso .... Open daily all year
Monteviot, Jedburgh .... 1 April - 31 October daily 12 - 5pm

STEWARTRY OF KIRKCUDBRIGHT

19 Rhonepark Crescent, Crossmichael .... *May - June by appointment*
Arndarroch Cottage, St John's Town of Dalry .. *July - Sept by appointment*
Barnhourie Mill, Colvend .... *May - Oct by appointment*
Carleton Croft, Borgue .... *July - August by appointment*
Corsock House, Castle Douglas .... *Apr - Jun by appt. (and for autumn colours)*
Danevale Park, Crossmichael .... *By appointment till 1 June*
Southwick House, Dumfries .... *Monday 26 - Friday 30 June*

STIRLING

14 Glebe Crescent, Tillicoultry .... *By appointment*
Arndean, Stirling .... *By appointment May and June*
Blairuskin Lodge, Kinlochard .... *By appointment*
Callander Lodge, Callander .... *By appointment April - End August*
Camallt, Fintry .... *By appointment*
Culbuie, Buchlyvie .... *Tues May -Oct 1 -5pm or by appointment*
Daldrishaig House, Aberfoyle .... *By appointment April, May, June & July*
Gargunnock House, Gargunnock .... *Weds mid April - mid June & in Sept & Oct*
.... *and by appointment*
Kilbryde Castle, Dunblane .... *By appointment*
The Cottage, Buchlyvie .... *By appointment weekdays May & June*

WIGTOWN

Ardwell House Gardens, Ardwell .... *Daily 1 April - 30 September 10am - 5pm*
Logan House Gardens, Port Logan .... *Daily 1 February - 1 April 10am - 4pm*
.... *2 April - 31 August 9am - 6pm*

MONTHLY LIST
FULL DETAILS ARE GIVEN IN THE DISTRICT LIST OF GARDENS

To be announced
Edinburgh & W. Lothian .... Dalmeny Park, South Queensferry
Stewartry of Kirkcudbright .... Danevale Park, Crossmichael

Sunday 19 February
Refrew & Inverclyde .... Ardgowan, Inverkip

Sunday 26 February
Ayrshire .... Blairquhan, Straiton, Maybole

Sunday 2 April
East Lothian .... Winton House, Pencaitland
Edinburgh & W. Lothian .... 61 Fountainhall Road, Edinburgh

Thursday 6 April
Ross,Cromarty,Skye & Inverness Dundonnell House, Dundonnell, Wester Ross

Sunday 9 April
Berwickshire .... Netherbyres, Eyemouth
Dumfries .... Dalswinton House, Auldgirth
Fife .... Wemyss Castle, Wemyss
Renfrew & Inverclyde .... Finlaystone, Langbank
Stewartry of Kirkcudbright .... Senwick House, Brighouse Bay
Stirling .... Camallt, Fintry

Saturday 15 April
Ross,Cromarty,Skye & Inverness Inverewe, Poolewe

Sunday 23 April
Argyll .... Benmore Botanic Garden, Dunoon
Dunbartonshire West .... Kilarden, Rosneath
Ettrick & Lauderdale .... Bemersyde, Melrose
Fife .... Spring Plant Fair, Cambo
Moray & Nairn .... Knocknagore, Knockando
Perth & Kinross .... Megginch Castle, Errol

Saturday 29 April
Argyll .... Strachur House Woodland Garden

Sunday 30 April
Argyll .... Strachur House Woodland Garden
East Lothian .... Shepherd House, Inveresk
Stewartry of Kirkcudbright .... Walton Park, Castle Douglas
Stirling .... The Pass House, Kilmahog

Saturday 6 May
Argyll .... Arduaine, Kilmelford

Sunday 7 May
Argyll .... Arduaine, Kilmelford
Argyll .... Crinan Hotel Garden, Crinan
Dumfries .... Portrack House, Holywood
Edinburgh & W. Lothian .... Belgrave Crescent Gardens
Edinburgh & W. Lothian .... Dean Gardens, Edinburgh
Fife .... Barham, The Bow of Fife
Fife .... Parleyhill Garden & Manse Garden, Culross
Perth & Kinross .... Branklyn, Perth
Perth & Kinross .... Glendoick, by Perth
Wigtown .... Logan House Garden, Port Logan

Sunday 14 May
Angus .... Brechin Castle, Brechin
Argyll .... Achara House, Duror of Appin
Berwickshire .... Charterhall, Duns
Dumfries .... Dalswinton House, Auldgirth
Dunbartonshire West .... Geilston Garden, Cardross
East Lothian .... Shepherd House, Inveresk
East Lothian .... Tyninghame House, Dunbar
Fife .... Micklegarth, Aberdour
Perth & Kinross .... Glendoick, by Perth
Perth & Kinross .... Rossie House, Forgandenny
Ross,Cromarty,Skye & Inverness Kilcoy Castle, Muir of Ord
Ross,Cromarty,Skye & Inverness The Hydroponicum, Achiltibuie
Stewartry of Kirkcudbright .... Danevale Park, Crossmichael
Stirling .... Kilbryde Castle, Dunblane (Gardeners' Market)
Wigtown .... Woodfall Gardens, Glasserton

Sunday 21 May

Dumfries	Peilton, Moniaive and Townhead of Glencairn
Dunbartonshire West	Ross Priory, Gartocharn
East Lothian	Stobshiel House, Humbie
Edinburgh & W. Lothian	61 Fountainhall Road, Edinburgh
Edinburgh & W. Lothian	Moray Place & Bank Gardens, Edinburgh
Fife	Kirklands, Saline
Perth & Kinross	Balnakeilly, Pitlochry
Renfrew & Inverclyde	Paisley Park Road Gardens
Stirling	Bridge of Allan Gardens
Tweeddale	Baddingsgill, West Linton

Saturday 27 May

Argyll	Strachur House Woodland Garden
Fife	Falkland Small Gardens

Sunday 28 May

Angus	Dalfruin, Kirriemuir
Argyll	Strachur House Woodland Garden
Ayrshire	Borlandhills, Dunlop
Berwickshire	Whitchester House
Dunbartonshire West	Shandon Gardens
East Lothian	Inwood, Carberry
Edinburgh & W. Lothian	Suntrap Edinburgh Horticultural & Garden Centre
Fife	Falkland Small Gardens
Fife	Gorno Grove House, by Strathmiglo
Fife	St Andrews Small Gardens
Kincardine & Deeside	Inchmarlo House Garden, Banchory
Lochaber,Badenoch & Strathspey	Aberarder, Kinlochlaggan
Lochaber,Badenoch & Strathspey	Aberarder, Kinlochlaggan
Lochaber,Badenoch & Strathspey	Ardverikie, Kinlochlaggan
Perth & Kinross	Cloan, by Auchterarder
Stewartry of Kirkcudbright	Corsock House, Castle Douglas
Tweeddale	Haystoun, Peebles
Wigtown	Logan Botanic Garden, Port Logan

Wednesday 31 May

Ross,Cromarty,Skye & Inverness	House of Gruinard, by Laide

Saturday 3 June
Ross,Cromarty,Skye & Inverness Attadale, Strathcarron

Sunday 4 June
Aberdeen .... Dunecht House Gardens, Dunecht
Aberdeen .... Gregellen, Banchory Devenick
Aberdeen .... Kildrummy Castle Gardens, Alford
Aberdeen .... Tillypronie, Tarland
Angus .... Cortachy Castle, Kirriemuir
Clydesdale .... Biggar Park, Biggar
Dumfries .... Glenae, Amisfield
East Lothian .... Stenton Village Gardens
Fife .... St Monans Small Gardens
Kincardine & Deeside .... The Burn House, Glenesk
Midlothian .... Auchindinny House, Penicuik
Perth & Kinross .... Bradystone House, Murthly
Refrew & Inverclyde .... Carruth, Bridge of Weir
Stewartry of Kirkcudbright .... Cally Gardens, Gatehouse of Fleet
Stirling .... Southwood, Southfield Crescent, Stirling
Tweeddale .... Hallmanor, Peebles

Wednesday 7 June
Ross,Cromarty,Skye & Inverness Dundonnell House, Dundonnell, Wester Ross

Saturday 10 June
Argyll .... Crarae Glen Garden, Inveraray
Caithness & Sutherland .... Amat, Ardgay
East Lothian .... Greywalls Hotel, Gullane
East Lothian .... Inveresk, Near Musselburgh
East Lothian .... Shepherd House, Inveresk
Edinburgh & W. Lothian .... Sawmill, Harburn
Fife .... Balcarres, Colinsburgh
Glasgow & District .... Glasgow Botanic Gardens
Lochaber,Badenoch & Strathspey Ard-Daraich, Ardgour

Sunday 11 June
Aberdeen .... Esslemont, Ellon
Angus .... Kinnaird Castle
Argyll .... Crarae Glen Garden, Inveraray
Ayrshire .... Avonhill Cottage, Drumclog
Caithness & Sutherland .... Amat, Ardgay

Dumfries .... Grovehill House
East Lothian .... Inveresk, Near Musselburgh
East Lothian .... Shepherd House, Inveresk
Fife .... Blebo, Craigs Village
Fife .... Micklegarth, Aberdour
Glasgow .... Kilsyth Gardens
Lochaber,Badenoch & Strathspey Ard-Daraich, Ardgour
Midlothian .... The Old Parsonage & Brae House
Moray & Nairn .... Carestown Steading, Deskford
Stirling .... Dunblane Gardens, Dunblane
Tweeddale .... Broughton Place Stable Cottages, Broughton
Tweeddale .... Stobo Water Garden, Stobo, Peebles

Saturday 17 June
East Lothian .... Dirleton Village
Midlothian .... Lasswade: 16 Kevock Road

Sunday 18 June
Clydesdale .... Dippoolbank Cottage, Carnwath
Dumfries .... Dunesslin, Dunscore
East Lothian .... Blackdykes, North Berwick
East Lothian .... Dirleton Village
Fife .... Freuchie Plant Sale
Fife .... Gattonside Village Gardens
Glagow .... 46 Corrour Road, Newlands
Midlothian .... Lasswade: 16 Kevock Road
Midlothian .... Newhall, Carlops
Perth & Kinross .... Explorers, The Scottish Plant Hunters Garden
Stirling .... Kilbryde Castle, Dunblane

Wednesday 21 June
Edinburgh .... 61 Fountainhall Road, Edinburgh

Thursday 22 June
Fife .... Myres Castle, by Auchtermuchty

Sunday 25 June
Aberdeen .... Howemill, Craigievar, Alford
Ayrshire .... Peatland, Gatehead
Caithness & Sutherland .... Sandside House, Reay
Clydesdale .... Baitlaws, Lamington

Dumfries .... The Garth, Tynron
East Lothian .... Tyninghame House, Dunbar
Edinburgh & W. Lothian .... Merchiston Cottage, 16 Colinton Road, Edinburgh
Edinburgh & W. Lothian .... Mo Runlion, Kirknewton
Ettrick & Lauderdale .... Gatonside Village Gardens
Fife .... Earlshall Castle, Leuchars
Fife .... Leckerston Cottage, Saline
Kincardine & Deeside .... Crathes Castle, Banchory
Perth & Kinross .... The Cottage, Longforgan
Renfrew & Inverclyde .... Lochwinnoch Gardens
Ross, Cromarty, Skye & Inverness House of Aigas and Field Centre, by Beauly
Stewartry of Kirkcudbright .... Southwick House, Dumfries
Stirling .... Thorntree, Arnprior
Tweeddale .... West Linton Village Gardens

Saturday 1 July
Argyll .... Strachur House Woodland Garden
Ayrshire .... Ladyburn, By Maybole
Caithness & Sutherland .... Dunrobin Castle & Gardens, Golspie

Sunday 2 July
Aberdeen .... Ploughmans Hall, Old Rayne
Angus .... Edzell Village
Argyll .... Strachur House Woodland Garden
Ayrshire .... Ladyburn, By Maybole
Berwickshire .... Antons Hill, Leitholm
Clydesdale .... 20 Smithycroft, Hamilton
Clydesdale .... Drakelaw Pottery, Crawfordjohn
Dumfries .... Ravenshill House Hotel, Lockerbie
East Lothian .... Gifford Village Gardens, North Berwick
Edinburgh .... South Queensferry Gardens
Ettrick & Lauderdale .... Crosslee Old Farmhouse, Ettrick Valley &
Netherpawhope
Fife .... Lathrisk House, Old Lathrisk & North Lodge, Freuchie
Isle of Arran .... Dougarie
Perth & Kinross .... Glenearn House, Bridge of Earn
Perth & Kinross .... Strathgarry House, Killiecrankie
Renfrew & Inverclyde .... Johnstone Gardens
Ross,Cromarty,Skye & Inverness Kilcoy Castle, Muir of Ord
Roxburgh .... Benrig, Benrig Cottage & Stable House
Stirling .... 14 Glebe Crescent, Tillicoultry
Tweeddale .... Drumelzier Old Manse, Broughton
Wigtown .... Craichlaw, Kirkcowan

Saturday 8 July

Edinburgh & W. Lothian .... Malleny Garden, Balerno
Midlothian .... Barondale House, Newbattle
Roxburgh .... Floors Castle, Kelso - Gardeners' Festival

Sunday 9 July

Aberdeen .... 23 Don Street, Old Aberdeen
Angus .... Gallery, Montrose
Ayrshire .... Penkhill Castle, Near Girvan
East Lothian .... Gateside House, Gullane
Fife .... Micklegarth, Aberdour
Fife .... Teasses, Nr Ceres
Kincardine & Deeside .... Findrack, Torphins
Midlothian .... Barondale House Newbattle
Midlothian .... Newhall, Carlops
Perth .... Wester Cloquhat, Bridge of Cally
Refrew & Inverclyde .... Houston Gardens
Ross,Cromarty,Skye & Inverness Novar, Evanton
Roxburgh .... Floors Castle, Kelso - Gardeners' Festival
Stewartry of Kirkcudbright .... Threave Garden, Castle Douglas
Stirling .... Gartmore Village
Wigtown .... Woodfall Gardens, Glasserton

Wednesday 12 July

Caithness & Sutherland .... The Castle & Gardens of Mey, Caithness

Saturday 15 July

Ayrshire .... Barr Village Gardens
Isle of Arran .... Brodick Castle & Country Park
Renfrew & Inverclyde .... Sma Shot Cottages Heritage Centre, Paisley

Sunday 16 July

Ayrshire .... Barr Village Gardens
Angus .... Glamis Castle, Glamis
Berwickshire .... Netherbyres, Eyemouth
Dumfries .... Cowhill Tower, Holywood
Fife .... Earlshall Castle, Leuchars
Fife .... Wormistoune, Crail
Kincardine & Deeside .... Drum Castle, Drumoak
Perth & Kinross .... Auchleeks House, Calvine
Roxburgh .... Corbet Tower, Morebattle

Thursday 20 July
Caithness & Sutherland .... The Castle & Gardens of Mey, Caithness

Saturday 22 July
Edinburgh & W. Lothian .... 2 Houstoun Gardens, Uphall
Fife .... Crail Small Gardens

Sunday 23 July
Aberdeen .... Leith Hall, Kennethmont
Ayrshire .... Carnell, Hurlford
Clydesdale .... Carnwath Village Gardens Trail
Edinburgh & W. Lothian .... 2 Houstoun Gardens, Uphall
Fife .... Crail Small Gardens
Kincardine & Deeside .... Douneside House, Tarland
Moray & Nairn .... Knocknagore, Knockando
Perth & Kinross .... Boreland, Killin
Ross, Cromarty, Skye & Inverness House of Aigas and Field Centre
Roxburgh .... West Leas, Bonchester Bridge
Stewartry of Kirkcudbright .... Millhouse, Rhonehouse
Stewartry of Kirkcudbright .... The Mill House, Gelston
Tweeddale .... West Linton Village Gardens

Saturday 29 July
Caithness & Sutherland .... House of Tongue, Tongue
Fife .... Strathkinness Village Gardens

Sunday 30 July
Argyll .... Ardchattan Priory Fete, North Connel
Ayrshire .... Skeldon, Dalrymple
Caithness & Sutherland .... Sandside House Gardens, by Reay, Thurso
Edinburgh & W. Lothian .... Annet House, Linlithgow
Fife .... Strathkinness Village Gardens
Refrew & Inverclyde .... Greenock West Gardens
Roxburgh .... St. Boswells Village
Stewartry of Kirkcudbright .... Arndarroch Cottage, St John's Town of Dalry

Saturday 5 August
Edinburgh & W. Lothian .... Dr Neil's Garden Trust, Duddingston

Sunday 6 August

Angus .... Redhall, Kirriemuir
Ayrshire .... Glendoune, Girvan
Caithness & Sutherland .... Langwell, Berriedale
Edinburgh & W. Lothian .... Dr Neil's Garden Trust, Duddingston
Kincardine & Deeside .... Glenbervie House, Drumlithie
Moray & Nairn .... Bents Green, 10 Pilmuir Road West, Forres
Midlothian .... Pomathorn Gardens, Nr. Penicuik
Perth & Kinross .... Cluniemore, Pitlochry
Perth & Kinross .... Drummond Castle Gardens, Muthill
Refrew & Inverclyde .... Barshaw Park, Paisley
Roxburgh .... Yetholm Village

Saturday 12 August

Isle of Arran .... Brodick Castle & Country Park

Sunday 13 August

Aberdeen .... Castle Fraser, Kemnay
Caithness & Sutherland .... Langwell, Berriedale
Clydesdale .... Culter Allers, Coulter
Ettrick & Lauderdale .... Old Tollhouse, Mountbenger, Yarrow
Stewartry of Kirkcudbright .... Cally Gardens, Gatehouse of Fleet

Thursday 17 August

Ross, Cromarty, Skye & Inverness Dundonnell House, Dundonnell, Wester Ross

Saturday 19 August

Caithness & Sutherland .... The Castle & Gardens of Mey, Caithness

Sunday 20 August

Fife .... Falkland Palace, Falkland
Fife .... Ladies Lake, St Andrews
Ross & Cromarty .... The Hydroponicum, Achiltibuie
Stewartry of Kirkcudbright .... Crofts, Kirkpatrick Durham Sunday 21 August

Sunday 27 August

Aberdeen .... Pitmedden Garden, Ellon
Aberdeen .... Tillypronie, Tarland

Sunday 3 September
Dunbartonshire West .... Hill House Plant Sale, Helensburgh
Edinburgh & W. Lothian .... 61 Fountainhall Road, Edinburgh
Renfrew & Inverclyde .... SGS Plant Sale, Finlaystone, Langbank
Tweeddale .... Broughton Place Stable Cottages, Broughton
Tweeddale .... Dawyck Botanic Garden, Stobo

Saturday 9 September
Stewartry of Kirkcudbright .... Arndarroch Cottage, St John's Town of Dalry

Sunday 10 September
Perth & Kinross .... Cherrybank Gardens, Perth
Ross,Cromarty,Skye & Inverness Inverewe, Poolewe
Stewartry of Kirkcudbright .... Arndarroch Cottage, St John's Town of Dalry

Sunday 17 September
Fife .... Cambo House, Kingsbarns

Sunday 8 October
Edinburgh & W. Lothian .... 61 Fountainhall Road, Edinburgh
Fife .... SGS Plant Sale & Fair, Hill of Tarvit

Saturday 14 October
East & Mid Lothian .... SGS 10th Anniversary Plant Sale, Near Pathhead

Sunday 15 October
Stirling .... Gargunnock House, Gargunnock

Sunday 3 December
Midlothian .... Rosecourt, Inveresk

PLANT SALES 2006
See District Lists for further details

Renfrew & Inverclyde
Carruth, Bridge of Weir
Sunday 4 June 2 - 5pm

Glasgow & District
Glasgow Botanic Gardens
Saturday 10 June 11am - 4pm

Fife
Cambo, Kingsbarns
Sunday 23 April 1 - 5pm

Fife
Freuchie Plant Sale
Sunday 18 June Noon - 4pm

Dunbartonshire West
Hill House, Helensburgh
Sunday 3 September 11am - 4pm

Renfrew & Inverclyde
Finlaystone, Langbank
Sunday 10 September 11.30am - 4pm

Fife
Hill of Tarvit, Cupar
Saturday 8 October 10.30 - 4pm

East & Midlothian
Oxenfoord Mains, Dalkeith
Saturday 14 October 9.30 am- 3.30pm

Stirling
Gargunnock House, Gargunnock
Sunday 15 October 2 - 5pm

ABERDEEN

District Organiser	**Mrs J Pilc**, 15 South Avenue, Cults, Aberdeen AB15 9LQ,
Area Organisers:	**Mrs S Callen,** Cults House, Cults Avenue, Aberdeen AB15 9TB
	Mrs F G Lawson, Asloun, Alford AB33 8NR
	Mrs A Robertson, Drumblade House, Huntly AB54 6ER
	Mrs F M K Tuck, Allargue House, Corgarff AB36 8YP
Hon. Treasurer:	**Mr J Ludlow**. St Nicholas House, Banchory AB31 5YT

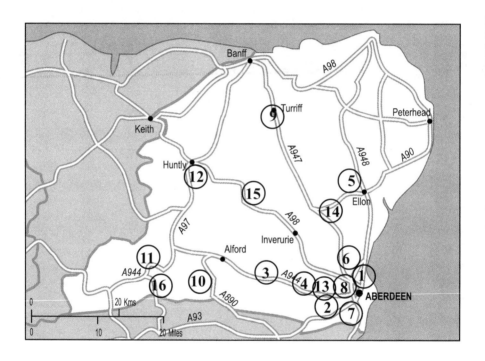

DATES OF OPENING

23 Don Street, Old Aberdeen .... June – August by appointment
Blairwood, Aberdeen .... Mid June - beginning Oct by appointment
Grandhome, Aberdeen .... By appointment
Greenridge, Cults .... July & August by appointment
Hatton Castle, Turriff .... By appointment
Howemill, Craigievar .... By appointment
Ploughman's Hall, Old Rayne .... By appointment

Dunecht House Gardens, Dunecht	Sunday 4 June	1 - 5pm
Kildrummy Castle Gardens, Alford	Sunday 4 June	10am - 5pm
Tillypronie, Tarland	Sunday 4 June	2 - 5pm
Esslemont, Ellon	Sunday 11 June	1 - 4.30pm
Howemill, Craigievar, Alford	Sunday 25 June	1.30 - 5pm
Ploughmans Hall, Old Rayne	Sunday 2 July	1 - 5pm
23 Don Street, Old Aberdeen	Sunday 9 July	1.30 - 6pm
Leith Hall, Kennethmont	Sunday 23 July	Noon - 5pm
Castle Fraser, Kemnay	Sunday 13 August	1 - 5pm
Pitmedden Garden, Ellon	Sunday 27 August	1 - 5pm
Tillypronie, Tarland	Sunday 27 August	2 - 5pm

1. 23 DON STREET, Old Aberdeen   ♿

(Miss M & Mr G Mackechnie)
Atmospheric walled garden in historic Old Aberdeen. Wide range of rare and unusual plants and old-fashioned scented roses. Full afternoon tea £2.00. Plant stall. Park at St Machar Cathedral, short walk down Chanonry to Don Street, turn right. City plan ref: P7.
Admission £2.50 Concessions £2.00
OPEN JUNE TO AUGUST BY APPOINTMENT Tel: 01224 487269.
SUNDAY 9 JULY 1.30 - 6pm
40% to Cat Protection   60% net to SGS Charities

2. BLAIRWOOD HOUSE, South Deeside Road, Blairs

(Ilse Elders)
Approximately a half acre country garden. Most of it started from scratch six years ago and still evolving. The garden has been self-designed to provide colour over a long season, without requiring daily care from the owner. Herbaceous borders, small beautiful herb garden packed with well over a hundred medicinal and culinary herbs, pebble mosaics and sunken patio area. (Very close to Blairs Museum) Teas and coffees available at Ardroe Hotel or The Old Mill Inn, just down the road. Route: Blairs, on the B9077, 5 mins by car from Bridge of Dee, Aberdeen.
Admission £2.50
BY APPOINTMENT MID JUNE to BEGINNING OF OCTOBER Tel: 01224 868301
40% to Aberdeen Greenbelt Alliance   60% net to SGS Charities

3. CASTLE FRASER, Kemnay   ♿

(The National Trust for Scotland)
Castle Fraser, one of the most spectacular of the Castles of Mar, built between 1575 and 1635 with designed landscape and parkland the work of Thomas White 1794. Includes an exciting new garden development within the traditional walled garden of cut flowers, trees, shrubs and new herbaceous borders. Also a medicinal and culinary border, organically grown fruit and vegetables and a newly constructed woodland garden with adventure playground. Plant and produce sales and home baked teas. Near Kemnay, off A944.
Admission £2.50 NTS members £1.50 and Children £1.00
SUNDAY 13 AUGUST 1 - 5pm
40% to The Gardens Fund of The National Trust for Scotland   60% net to SGS Charities
For other opening details see NTS advert at the back of the book

4. DUNECHT HOUSE GARDENS, Dunecht   ♿ (partly)

(The Hon. Charles A Pearson)

A magnificent copper beech avenue leads to Dunecht House built by John and William Smith with a Romanesque addition in 1877 by G Edmund Street. Highlights include rhododendrons, azaleas and a wildflower garden. Teas. Cars free. Dunecht 1 mile, routes: A944 and B977.
Admission £3.00 Concessions £1.50

SUNDAY 4 JUNE 1 - 5pm

40% to Riding for the Disabled 60% net to SGS Charities

---

5. ESSLEMONT, Ellon

(Mr & Mrs Wolrige Gordon of Esslemont)

Victorian house set in wooded policies above River Ythan. Roses and shrubs in garden with double yew hedges (17th and 18th centuries). Music, stalls, charity stalls, tombola. Home baked teas. Ellon 2 miles. Route: A920 from Ellon. On Pitmedden/Oldmeldrum road.
Admission: £2.00 Children (4 – 11 years) & Concessions £1.00

SUNDAY 11 JUNE 1 - 4.30pm

40% to Conerstone Community Care 60% net to SGS Charities

---

6. GRANDHOME, Aberdeen   ♿

(Mr & Mrs D R Paton)

18th century walled garden, incorporating rose garden; policies with rhododendrons, azaleas, mature trees and shrubs. Depending on the time of year, plants, fruit or vegetables may be available to buy. Route: from north end of North Anderson Drive, continue on A90 over Persley Bridge, turning left at Tesco roundabout. No dogs please.
Admission £2.50 Teas by arrangement

OPEN BY APPOINTMENT Tel: 01224 722 202

40% to Children First 60% net to SGS Charities

---

7. GREGELLEN HOUSE, Banchory Devenick, Aberdeenshire

(Mr & Mrs McGregor)

Former Victorian manse set in 1½ acres of garden. Herbaceous borders, lawns and rockeries with a wide and varied range of interesting plants which include azaleas, meconopsis, peonies and rhododendrons, making a colourful display. Teas and plant stall. Route: Approximately 1 - ¾ of a mile from Bridge of Dee off the B9077 South Deeside road.
Admission: £2.50 Children 50p

OPEN BY APPOINTMENT DURING MAY & JUNE

40% to Marie Curie Cancer Care 60% net to SGS Charities

---

8. GREENRIDGE, Craigton Road, Cults

(BP Exploration)

Large secluded garden surrounding 1840 Archibald Simpson house, for many years winner of Britain in Bloom 'Best Hidden Garden'. Mature specimen trees and shrubs. Sloping walled rose garden and terraces. Kitchen garden. Teas. Route: directions with booking.
Admission £3.50 including tea

JULY & AUGUST BY APPOINTMENT. Tel: 01224 860200 Fax: 01224 860210

40% to Association of the Friends of Raeden 60% net to SGS Charities

---

9. HATTON CASTLE, Turriff   ♿ with help
(Mr & Mrs James Duff)
Two acre walled garden featuring mixed borders and shrub roses with yew and box hedges and allees of pleached hornbeam. Kitchen garden and fan trained fruit trees. Lake and woodland walks. Afternoon tea and lunch parties by appointment. On A947 2 miles south of Turriff. Admission £4.50 Children free
OPEN BY APPOINTMENT
Tel: 01888 562279 Fax: 01888 563943 Email - *jjdgardens@btinternet.com*
40% to Future Hope 60% net to SGS Charities

10. HOWEMILL, Craigievar   ♿ with help
(Mr D Atkinson)
Maturing garden with a wide range of unusual alpines, shrubs and herbaceous plants. Plant stall. Teas. From Alford take A980 Alford/Lumphanan road. No dogs please. Admission £2.50 Children under 12 free
SUNDAY 25 JUNE 1.30 - 5pm OR BY APPOINTMENT. Tel: 01975 581278.
40% to Cancer Relief Macmillan Fund 60% net to SGS Charities

11. KILDRUMMY CASTLE GARDENS, Alford   ♿ (with help)
(Kildrummy Garden Trust)
April shows the gold of the lysichitons in the water garden, and the small bulbs naturalised beside the copy of the 14th century Brig o' Balgownie. Rhododendrons and azaleas from April (frost permitting). September/October brings colchicums and brilliant colour with acers, fothergillas and viburnums. Plants for sale. Play area. Tea room. Wheelchair facilities. Car park free inside hotel main entrance. Coach park up hotel delivery entrance. Parties by arrangement. *www.kildrummy-castle-gardens.co.uk* Open daily April - October. Tel: 01975 571277/571203. On A97, 10 miles from Alford, 17 miles from Huntly. Admission £3.00 Children free
SUNDAY 4 JUNE 10am - 5pm
40% to Marie Curie Cancer Care 60% net to SGS Charities

12. LEITH HALL, Kennethmont
(The National Trust for Scotland)
This attractive old country house, the earliest part of which dates from 1650, was the home of the Leith and Leith-Hay families for more than three centuries. The west garden was made by Mr and The Hon. Mrs Charles Leith-Hay around the beginning of the twentieth century. The property was given to the Trust in 1945. The rock garden has been enhanced by the Scottish Rock Garden Club in celebration of their 150th anniversary. Toilet for disabled visitors. Cream teas. Pipe band. Plant sales. Walks with the Head Gardener. On B9002 near Kennethmont. Plants for sale. Admission House - £7.00 Concs & Children £5.25 Garden - £2.50 Concs & Children £1.90
SUNDAY 23 JULY Noon - 5pm
40% to The Gardens Fund of The National Trust for Scotland 60% net to SGS Charities

13. LOCHAN HOUSE, Blackchambers, nr Blackburn ♿ (with help)

(Mrs M Jones)

Evolving country garden of 1½ acres. Includes ponds, and waterfowl collection, Herbacious plantings, formal courtyard and ornamental grass garden. Recently planted wildlife shelterbelt with paths and fine views to Bennachie. Teas. Route: A96 2 miles south of Kinellar roundabout, follow signs for Millbuie.

Admission £3.00 Accompanied children free.

GROUPS BY APPOINTMENT TEL: 01224 791753

40% to Breast Cancer Research, Aberdeen 60% net to SGS Charities

---

14. PITMEDDEN GARDEN, Ellon ♿

(The National Trust for Scotland)

Garden created by Lord Pitmedden in 1675. Elaborate floral designs in parterres of box edging, inspired by the garden at the Palace of Holyroodhouse, have been re-created by the Trust. Fountains and sundials make fine centrepieces to the garden, filled in summer with 40,000 annual flowers. Also herb garden, herbaceous borders, trained fruit, plant sales, Museum of Farming Life, Visitor Centre, nature hut, woodland walk and wildlife garden. Tearoom. Special rates for pre-booked coach parties.

Admission £5.00 Concessions & children £4.00

SUNDAY 27 AUGUST 1 - 5pm

40% to The Gardens Fund of The National Trust for Scotland 60% net to SGS Charities

---

15. PLOUGHMAN'S HALL, Old Rayne ♿ with help

(Mr & Mrs A Gardner)

One acre garden. Rock, herbaceous, kitchen, herb and woodland gardens. Plant and craft stalls. Off A96, 9 miles north of Inverurie.

Admission £2.00 Children 50p

SUNDAY 2 JULY 1 - 6pm also open by appointment Tel: 01464 851253

40% to Wycliffe Bible Translators 60% net to SGS Charities

---

16. TILLYPRONIE, Tarland ♿

(The Hon Philip Astor)

Late Victorian house for which Queen Victoria laid foundation stone. Herbaceous borders, terraced garden, heather beds, water garden and new rockery. New Golden Jubilee garden still being laid out. Shrubs and ornamental trees, including pinetum with rare specimens. Fruit garden and greenhouses. Superb views. Home-made teas. Plant sale - June opening only. Free car park. Dogs on lead, please. Between Ballater and Strathdon, off A97.

Admission £3.00 Children £1.50

SUNDAY 4 JUNE 2 - 5pm - Wonderful show of azaleas and spring heathers

SUNDAY 27 AUGUST 2 - 5pm

All proceeds to Scotland's Gardens Scheme

ANGUS

District Organiser: **Mrs Nici Rymer,** Nether Finlarg, Forfar DD8 1XQ

Area Organisers: **Miss Ruth Dundas,** Caddam, Kinnordy, Kirriemuir DD8 4LP
Mrs J Henderson, Mains of Panmuir, by Carnoustie DD7
Mrs R Porter, West Scryne, By Carnoustie DD7 6LL
Mrs C Smoor, Gagie House, Tealing, Dundee DD4 0PR
Mrs G Stewart, Ugiebank, Edzell
Mrs A Stormonth Darling, Lednathie, Glen Prosen Kirriemuir DD8

Hon. Treasurer: **Col R H B Learoyd,** Priestoun, Edzell DD9 7UD

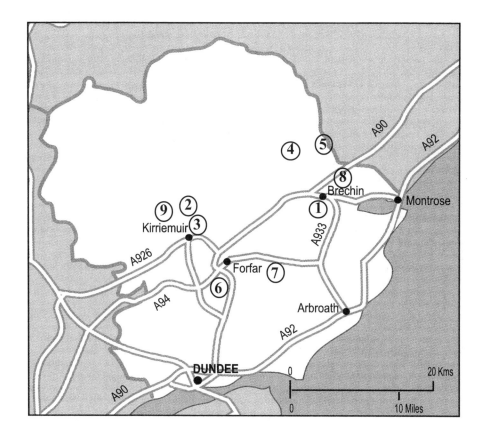

DATES OF OPENING

House of Pitmuies, Guthrie, By Forfar .... 1 April - 31 October   10am - 5pm

Brechin Castle, Brechin	Sunday 14 May	2 - 5.30pm
Dalfruin, Kirriemuir	Sunday 28 May	2 - 5pm
Cortachy Castle, Kirriemuir	Sunday 4 June	2 - 6pm
Kinnaird Castle.	Sunday 11 June	2 - 5pm
Edzell Village	Sunday 2 July	2 - 5pm
Gallery, Montrose	Sunday 9 July	2 - 5pm
Glamis Castle, Glamis	Sunday 16 July	10am - 6pm
Redhall.	Sunday 6 August	2 - 5pm

1. BRECHIN CASTLE, Brechin
(The Earl & Countess of Dalhousie)
Ancient fortress of Scottish kings on cliff overlooking River Southesk. Rebuilt by Alexander Edward – completed in 1711. Extensive walled garden 300 yards from Castle with ancient and new plantings and mown lawn approach. Rhododendrons, azaleas, bulbs, interesting trees, wild garden. Tea in garden. Car parking free. Route: A90, Brechin 1 mile.
Admission £2.50 Children 50p
SUNDAY 14 MAY 2 - 5.30pm
20% to Dalhousie Day Centre   20% to Unicorn Preservation Society   60% net to SGS Charities

2. CORTACHY CASTLE, Kirriemuir
(The Earl & Countess of Airlie)
16th century castellated house. Additions in 1872 by David Bryce. Spring garden and wild pond garden with azaleas, primroses and rhododendrons. Garden of fine American specie trees and river walk along South Esk. Teas. Plant sale and plant raffle, children's quiz.
Kirriemuir 5 miles. Route B955.
Admission £2.50 Children 50p
SUNDAY 4 JUNE 2 - 6pm
40% to Strathmore Hospice - Luppen Care   60% net to SGS Charities

3. DALFRUIN, Kirktonhill Road, Kirriemuir   ♿ (with assistance – grass paths just wide enough)
(Mr & Mrs James A Welsh)
A well-stocked mature garden of almost one-third of an acre situated at end of cul-de-sac. Unusual plants, dactylorhiza, tree peonies, meconopsis, trilliums. Stream added in Autumn 2000 (Newts first seen autumn 2003!). Good plant stall. No dogs please. Unless disabled please park on Roods or at St Mary's Church. From centre of Kirriemuir turn left up Roods; Kirktonhill Road is on left near top of hill, just before the school 20mph zone.
Admission £2.50 Accompanied children free Teas at St Mary's Church. Plant stall.
SUNDAY 28 MAY 2 - 5pm
20% to The Glens & Kirriemuir Old Parish Church   20% St Mary's Scottish Episcopal Church 60% net to SGS Charities

4. EDZELL VILLAGE

Walk round 10 gardens in Edzell village. Teas extra. Tickets are on sale in the village and a plan is issued with the tickets.

Admission £2.50 Children 50p

SUNDAY 2 JULY 2 - 5pm

40% to Strachathan Cancer Care Fund UK 60% net to SGS Charities

5. GALLERY, Montrose

(Mr & Mrs John Simson)

Redesign and replanting of this historic garden have preserved and extended its traditional framework of holly, privet and box. A grassed central alley, embellished with circles, links interesting theme gardens and lawns. A short walk leads to the raised bank of the North River Esk with views towards the Howe of the Mearns. From that point rough paths lead west and east along the bank. Route: From A90 immediately south of Northwater Bridge take exit to 'Hillside' and next left to 'Gallery & Marykirk'. Or from A937 immediately west of rail underpass follow signs to 'Gallery & Northwater Bridge'.

Admission £2.50 Children 50p

SUNDAY 9 JULY 2 - 5pm

40% to Practical Action 60% net to SGS Charities

6. GLAMIS CASTLE, Glamis ♿

(The Earl of Strathmore & Kinghorne)

Family home of the Earls of Strathmore and a royal residence since 1372. Childhood home of HM Queen Elizabeth The Queen Mother, birthplace of HRH The Princess Margaret, and legendary setting for Shakespeare's play 'Macbeth'. Five-storey L-shaped tower block dating from 15th century, remodelled 1600, containing magnificent rooms with wide range of historic pictures, furniture, porcelain etc. Spacious grounds with river and woodland walks through pinetum and nature trail. Walled garden exhibition. Formal garden. For this day only the greenhouses and famous vine collection will be open. Restaurant. Teas. Shopping pavilion. Glamis 1 mile A94.

Admission to Castle & grounds: £7.30, OAPs £6.10, Children £4.10

Admission: Grounds only £3.70 Children & OAPs £2.70

SUNDAY 16 JULY 10am - 6pm

40% to Princess Royal Trust for Carers 60% net to SGS Charities

7. HOUSE OF PITMUIES, Guthrie, By Forfar

(Mrs Farquhar Ogilvie)

Two semi-formal wall gardens adjoin 18th century house and shelter long borders of herbaceous perennials, superb delphiniums, old fashioned roses and pavings with violas and dianthus. Spacious lawns, river and lochside walks beneath fine trees. A wide variety of shrubs with good autumn colours. Massed spring bulbs, interesting turreted doocot and "Gothick" wash-house. Dogs on lead please. Rare and unusual plants for sale. Fruit in season. Friockheim 1½ miles. Route A932.

Admission £2.50

1 APRIL - 31 OCTOBER 10am - 5pm

Donations to Scotland's Gardens Scheme

8. KINNAIRD CASTLE
(Earl & Countess of Southesk)
Formal yew terrace and recently planted shrub garden. Rhododendrons and woodland walks.
Deer Park. Teas. Take A933 Arbroath road out of Brechin, follow signs for Kinnaird Park.
Admission £2.50 Children 50p
SUNDAY 11 JUNE 2 – 5pm
40% to Brechin Youth Project   60% net to SGS Charities

---

9. REDHALL, Kirriemuir
(Mr & Mrs Bolt)
An informal, one acre country garden with broad borders of viburnums, euronymus and other
shrubs. Some interesting trees including a collection of over sixty species and cultivars of rowan.
A wildlife pond, peafowl and scots dumpies mean that only guide dogs are allowed. Route: from
Kirriemuir take the B9555 for Dykehead, Prosem, Clova. Visit www.redhall.org.uk for more
information. Teas. Plant stall.
Admission £2.50 Children 50p if accompanied.
SUNDAY 6 AUGUST 2 - 5pm
40% to Perennial 60% net to SGS Charities

ARGYLL

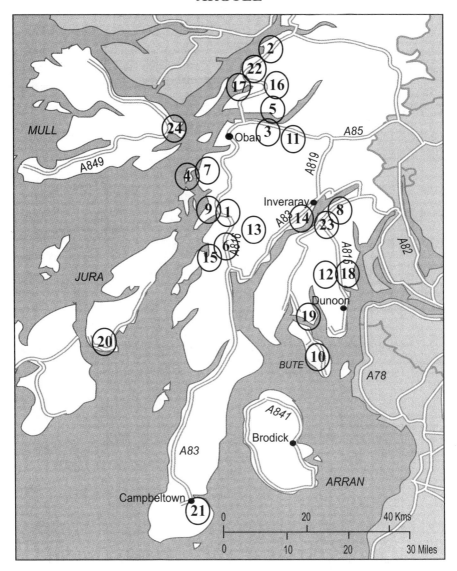

District Organiser	**Mrs C Struthers**, Ardmaddy Castle, Balvicar PA34 4QY
& Hon Treasurer:	
Area Organisers:	**Mrs G Cadzow**, Duachy, Kilninver, Oban PA34 4RH
	Mrs E B Ingleby, Braighbhaille, Crarae, Inveraray PA32 8YA
	Mrs P Lang, Ardrannoch, Ledaig PA37 1QU
	Mrs M Thomson, Glenbranter House, By Strachur, Argyll PA27 8DJ

DATES OF OPENING

26 Kilmartin, Lochgilphead	1 June - 30 September	10.30am - Dusk
Achnacloich, Connel..	Daily 8 April - 31 October	10am - 6pm
An Cala, Ellenabeich	Daily 1 April - 31 October	10am - 6pm
Ardchattan Priory, North Connel	Daily 1 April - 31 October	9am - 6pm
Ardkinglas Woodland Garden.	Daily all year	daylight hours
Ardmaddy Castle, by Oban	Daily all year	9am - sunset
	or by appointment	
Ascog Hall, Isle of Bute	Daily (except Mons & Tues)	
	Easter - End October	10am - 5pm
Ardnow, Cairndow	By appointment	
Barguillean's "Angus Garden" .	Daily all year	9am - 6pm
Cnoc-na-Garrie, Ballymeanoch	By appointment April - Sept	
Druimavuic House, Appin	Daily April, May & June	10am - 6pm
Druimneil House, Port Appin.	Daily 1 April - 31 October	9am - 6pm
Eckford, By Dunoon	Daily 9 April - 6 June	10am - 5pm
Glecknabae, Isle of Bute	By appointment Spring - Autumn	
Jura House, Ardfin, Isle of Jura	Open all year	9am - 5pm
Kildalloig, Campbeltown.	By appointment	
Kinlochlaich House Gardens, Appin	Open all year	9.30 -5.30 or dusk
(Except Sunday's October - March) Sunday's April - September		10.30am - 5.30pm
Torosay Castle Gardens, Isle of Mull	Open all year	

Benmore Botanic Garden, Dunoon	Sunday 23 April	10am - 6pm
Strachur House Woodland Garden	Sat & Sun 29 & 30 April	1 - 5pm
Arduaine, Kilmelford	Sat & Sun 6 & 7 May	9.30am - 6pm
Crinan Hotel Garden, Crinan	Sunday 7 May	Noon - 5pm
Achara House, Duror of Appin.	Sunday 14 May	2 - 6pm
Strachur House Woodland Garden	Sat & Sun 27 & 28 May	1- 5pm
Crarae Garden, Inveraray	Sat & Sun 10 & 11 June	9.30am - 6pm
Strachur House Woodland Garden	Sat & Sun 1 & 2 July	1- 5pm
Ardchattan Priory Fete, Connel	Sunday 30 July	Noon - 4pm

1. 26 KILMARTIN, Lochgilphead   ♿ (partially)

(Mrs M A Rayner)

Mixed borders, roses, perennials, large rock garden, wild garden, snowdrops, bulbs, trees, azaleas and rhododendrons. Steps to burn. Free range hens. Play area. Plant stall.

Route: A82 - 8 miles north of Lochgilphead in village of Kilmartin.

Admission £2.50

OPEN 10.30am - DUSK 1 JUNE - 30 SEPTEMBER

40% between Zambesi Mission and Mid Argyll Link CLub 60% net to SGS Charities

2. ACHARA HOUSE, Duror of Appin &

(Mr & Mrs Alastair Macpherson of Pitmain)
A recently created garden set round the attractive Achara House (attributed to Robert Lorimer), containing an extensive collection of rhododendron species and hybrids, azaleas and camellias. Hill garden with fine view of Loch Linnhe. Teas. On A828 just south of Duror, 7 miles south of Ballachulish Bridge and 5 miles north of Appin.
Admission £2.00 Children free
SUNDAY 14 MAY 2 - 6pm
40% to Cancer Relief Macmillan Fund 60% net to SGS Charities

---

3. ACHNACLOICH, Connel &

(Mrs T E Nelson)
Scottish baronial house by John Starforth of Glasgow. Succession of bulbs, flowering shrubs, rhododendrons, azaleas, magnolias and primulas. Woodland garden with ponds above Loch Etive. Good Autumn colours. Plants for sale. Dogs on lead please. On the A85 3 miles east of Connel.
Admission £2.00   Children free OAPs £1.00
DAILY 8 APRIL - 31 OCTOBER 10am - 6pm
All takings to Scotland's Gardens Scheme

---

4. AN CALA, Ellenabeich, Isle of Seil

(Mrs Thomas Downie)
A small garden of under five acres designed in the 1930s, An Cala sits snugly in its horse-shoe shelter of surrounding cliffs. A very pretty garden with streams, waterfall, ponds, many herbaceous plants as well as azaleas, rhododendrons and cherry trees in spring. Proceed south from Oban on Campbeltown road for 8 miles, turn right at Easdale sign, a further 8 miles on B844; garden between school and village.
Admission £2.50 Children free
DAILY FROM 1 APRIL - 31 OCTOBER 10am - 6pm
Donation to Scotland's Gardens Scheme

---

5. ARDCHATTAN PRIORY, North Connel &

(Mrs Sarah Troughton)
Beautifully situated on the north side of Loch Etive. The Priory, founded in 1230, is now a private house. The ruins of the chapel and graveyard, with fine early stones, are in the care of Historic Scotland and open with the garden. The front of the house has a rockery, extensive herbaceous and rose borders, with excellent views over Loch Etive. To the west of the house there are shrub borders and a wild garden, numerous roses and over 30 different varieties of Sorbus providing excellent autumn colour. Oban 10 miles. From north, turn left off A828 at Barcaldine on to B845 for 6 miles. From Oban or the east on A85, cross Connel Bridge and turn first right, proceed east on Bonawe Road. Well signed.
Admission £2.50 Children free
DAILY FROM 1 APRIL - 31 OCTOBER 9am - 6pm
A fete will be held on SUNDAY 30 JULY Noon - 4pm
Donation to Scotland's Gardens Scheme

---

6. ARDKINGLAS WOODLAND GARDEN, Cairndow

(Ardkinglas Estate)

In peaceful setting overlooking Loch Fyne the garden contains one of the finest collections of rhododendrons and conifers in Britain. This includes the mightiest conifer in Europe and one of Britain's tallest trees as well as many other champion trees. Gazebo with unique "Scriptorium" based around a collection of literary quotes. Woodland lochan, ancient mill ruins and many woodland walks. Plant and gift sales, picnic facilities, car park and toilets. Dogs allowed on a lead. Entrance through Cairndow village off A83 Loch Lomond/Inveraray road. Admission £3.00 Children under 16 years free. Scottish Tourist Board 3* Garden.

OPEN DAYLIGHT HOURS ALL YEAR ROUND

Donation to Scotland's Gardens Scheme

---

7. ARDMADDY CASTLE, Balvicar, by Oban   ♿ (mostly)

(Mr & Mrs Charles Struthers)

Ardmaddy Castle, with its woodlands and formal walled garden on one side and spectacular views to the islands and the sea on the other, has many fine rhododendrons and azaleas with a variety of trees, shrubs, unusual vegetables and flower borders between dwarf box hedges. Daffodils and bluebell woods. Recently created water gardens and stoneworks add increasing interest to this continuously developing garden. Sales area with many unusual plants and shrubs, and veg and fruit when available. Toilet (suitable for disabled). Oban 13 miles, Easdale 3 miles. 1½ miles of narrow road off B844 to Easdale.

Admission £2.50 Children 50p

DAILY ALL YEAR 9am - sunset

Other visits by arrangement: Tel. 01852 300353

Donations to Scotland's Gardens Scheme

---

8. ARDNO, Cairndow

(Kate How)

Begun in 1992 - an overgrown canvas in need of extensive clearing. 12 years on it is becoming well established with interesting trees and shrubs around the house, through the beautiful wooded gorge and down to the Loch via the meadow/arboretum. The site is stunning and the garden is maturing amazingly quickly. Interesting for those planning to start from scratch! Situated at the top end of Loch Fyne betweeen Cairndow and St Catherines, off the A815. Admission £2.50 Children free

OPEN BY APPOINTMENT Tel: 01499 302304 - Michael & Karen Bowyer

40% to S J Noble Trust   60% net to SGS Charities

---

9. ARDUAINE, Kilmelford   ♿

(The National Trust for Scotland)

An outstanding 20 acre coastal garden on the Sound of Jura. Begun more than 100 years ago on the south facing slope of a promontory separating Asknish Bay from Loch Melfort, this remarkable hidden paradise, protected by tall shelterbelts and influenced favourably by the Gulf Stream, grows a wide variety of plants from the four corners of the globe. Internationally known for the rhododendron species collection, the garden also features magnolias, camellias, azaleas and many other wonderful trees and shrubs, many of which are tender and not often seen. A broad selection of perennials, bulbs, ferns and water plants ensure a year-long season of interest. Route: Off the A816 Oban - Lochgilphead, sharing an entrance with the Loch Melfort Hotel. Admission Adults £5.00 Concessions £4.00 Under 5s free Family £14.00

SATURDAY & SUNDAY 6 & 7 MAY 9.30am - 6pm

40% to The Gardens Fund of The National Trust for Scotland   60% net to SGS Charities

---

10. ASCOG HALL, Ascog, Isle of Bute
(Mr & Mrs W Fyfe)
Recently restored after decades of neglect, this appealing garden is continuing to develop and mature, with an abundance of choice plants and shrubs which delight the eye from spring to autumn. It includes a formal rose garden with a profusion of fragrant old shrub roses. Through a rustic ivy-clad stone arch which in bygone years led to the tennis court. There is now a large gravel garden with sun-loving plants and grasses. Undoubtedly, however, the most outstanding feature is our acclaimed Victorian fernery. This rare and beautiful structure houses subtropical and temperate fern species, including an ancient Todea barbara - the only survivor from the original collection, and said to be around 1,000 years old. Plant Stall.
Admission £3.00 Children free, under supervision. Sorry no dogs.
OPEN DAILY (Except Mons & Tues) EASTER - END OCTOBER 10am - 5pm
Donation to Scotland's Gardens Scheme

---

11. BARGUILLEAN'S "ANGUS GARDEN", Taynuilt
(Mr Robin Marshall)
Nine acre woodland garden around an eleven acre loch set in the Glen Lonan hills. Spring flowering shrubs and bulbs, extensive collection of rhododendron hybrids, deciduous azaleas, primulas, conifers and unusual trees. The garden contains a large collection of North American rhododendron hybrids from famous comtemporary plant breeders. Some paths can be steep. 3 marked walks from 30 minutes to 1½ hours. Coach tours by arrangement. Contact Sean Honeyman Tel 01866 822 335 Route: 3 miles south off A85 Glasgow/Oban road at Taynuilt; road marked Glen Lonan; 3 miles up single track road; turn right at sign.
Admission £2.00 Children free
DAILY ALL YEAR 9am - 6pm
Donation to Scotland's Gardens Scheme

---

12. BENMORE BOTANIC GARDEN, Dunoon ♿ (limited due to hill slopes)
(Regional Garden of the Royal Botanic Garden Edinburgh and one of the National Botanic Gardens of Scotland)
World famous for its magnificent conifers and its extensive range of flowering trees and shrubs, including over 250 species of rhododendron. From a spectacular avenue of Giant Redwoods, numerous waymarked walks lead the visitor via a formal garden and pond through hillside woodlands to a dramatic viewpoint overlooking the Eachaig valley and the Holy Loch. James Duncan Cafe (licensed) and Botanics Shop for gifts and plants. Also newly renovated Courtyard Gallery with events and exhibitions. Dogs permitted on a short leash. 7 miles north of Dunoon or 22 miles south from Glen Kinglass below Rest and Be Thankful pass; on A815.
Admission £3.50 Concessions £3.00 Children £1.00 Families £8.00
SUNDAY 23 APRIL 10am - 6pm
Donation to Scotland's Gardens Scheme
For further details see advert at back of book

Why not look up the gardens on our website?
www.gardensofscotland.org
PHOTOS AND MAPS

13. CNOC-NA-GARRIE, Ballymeanoch, by Lochgilphead
(Mrs Dorothy Thomson)
A garden being created from rough hillside, designed for year-round interest. Large range of alpines, shrubs, grasses, herbaceous plants and bulbs, many grown from seed. Plant stall. 2 miles south of Kilmartin, A816. Entrance sharp left between cottages and red brick house, continue up track to bungalow. No dogs please.
Admission £2.50 Accompanied children free.
OPEN APRIL - SEPTEMBER OR BY APPOINTMENT TEL: 01546 605327
20% to British Red Cross Society (mid Argyll)   20% to Cancer Relief Macmillan Fund 60% net to SGS Charities

---

14. CRARAE GARDEN, Inveraray   ♿ (only Lower Gardens)
(The National Trust for Scotland)
A spectacular 50 acre garden in a dramatic setting. Crarae has a wonderful collection of woody plants centered on the Crarae Burn, which is spanned by several bridges and tumbles through a rocky gorge in a series of cascades. A wide variety of shrubs and trees, chosen for spring flowering and autumn colour grow in the shelter of towering conifers and the lush, naturalistic planting and rushing water gives the garden the feel of a valley in the Himalayas. Sturdy shoes advised. 11 miles south of Inverarary / 14 miles north of Lochgilphead on A83.
Dogs permitted on a short lead only.
Admission £5.00 Concessions £4.00 Under 5s free Family £14.00 (Correct at time of going to press)
SATURDAY & SUNDAY 10 & 11 JUNE 9.30am - 6pm
Donation to Scotland's Gardens Scheme

---

15. CRINAN HOTEL GARDEN, Crinan
(Mr & Mrs N Ryan)
Small rock garden with azaleas and rhododendrons created into a steep hillside over a century ago with steps leading to a sheltered, secluded garden with sloping lawns, herbaceous beds and spectacular views of the canal and Crinan Loch. Lochgilphead A83, then A816 to Oban, then A841 Cairnbaan to Crinan. Raffle of a painting of flowers by Frances Macdonald. Teas at coffee shop beside canal basin.
Admission £2.00 Accompanied children free
SUNDAY 7 MAY Noon - 5pm
40% to Feedback Madagascar   60% net to SGS Charities

---

16. DRUIMAVUIC HOUSE, Appin
(Mr & Mrs Newman Burberry)
Stream, wall and woodland gardens with lovely views over Loch Creran. Spring bulbs, rhododendrons, azaleas, primulas, meconopsis, violas. Dogs on lead please. Plant stall. Route A828 Oban/Fort William, 4 miles south of Appin. At either end of new bridge bear left at roundabout. At the north end road is signed Invercreran, at the south end road is signed "Local Traffic". Two miles from either end, look for private road where public signs warn of flooding.
Admission £2.00 Children free
DAILY APRIL, MAY & JUNE 10am - 6pm
30% to Alzheimer Scotland - Action on Dementia (Oban & Lorne Branch) 70% net to SGS Charities

17. DRUIMNEIL HOUSE, Port Appin

(Mrs J Glaisher)

Gardener - Mr Andrew Ritchie

Ten acre garden overlooking Loch Linnhe with many fine varieties of mature trees and rhododendrons and other woodland shrubs. Home made teas available. Turn in Appin off A828 (Connel/Fort William road). 2 miles, sharp left at Airds Hotel, second house on right. Lunches by prior arrangement. Tel: 01631 730228. Plants for sale. Sorry no dogs.
Donations
OPEN DAILY 1 APRIL - 31 OCTOBER 9am - 6pm
All takings to Scotland's Gardens Scheme

---

18. ECKFORD, By Dunoon

(Mr D Younger)

For many years closely connected with the Benmore Botanic Garden, Eckford has a 4 acre woodland garden of immense charm sited on a hillside. The general public will enjoy the massed blooms of rhododendrons and azaleas, and the specialist gardener will notice unusual specimens of trees and shrubs that have been planted over the past 100 years. This is a wild garden, so sturdy shoes are advised. Eckford lies just off the A815 about 6½ miles north of Dunoon and ½ mile south of Benmore Garden. Plants for sale when available.
Admission £2.50
OPEN DAILY FROM 9 APRIL - 6 JUNE 10am - 5pm
40% to John Younger Trust   60% net to SGS Charities

---

19. GLECKNABAE, Rothesay   ♿ (partially)

(Iain & Margaret Gimblett)

A south-facing hillside garden in the least known part of the island of Bute with magnificent views to the mountains of Arran. A collection of formal courtyard gardens, all different, with rock, boulder and bog gardens as well as shrubs and trees. This unusual garden is welcoming and inspirational. Route: A844 to Ettrick Bay, signposted off the coast road between Rhubodach and Rothesay; continue to end of 'made up' road; approximately 5 miles. A 'music in the garden' day is planned for Sunday 25 June 2-5pm - watch the web site for further details.
By appointment from Spring to Autumn Tel: 01700 505655 E-mail: gimblettsmill@aol.com
Individuals or small parties welcome
Donations 40% to The British Heart Foundation   60% net to SGS Charities

---

20. JURA HOUSE, Ardfin, Isle of Jura

(The Ardfin Trust)

Organic walled garden with wide variety of unusual plants and shrubs, including large Australasian collection. Also interesting woodland and cliff walk, spectacular views. Points of historical interest, abundant wild life and flowers. Plant stall. Tea tent June, July and August. Toilet. 5 miles east from ferry terminal on A846. Ferries to Islay from Kennacraig by Tarbert.
Admission £2.50 Students £1.00 Children up to 16 free
OPEN ALL YEAR 9am - 5pm
Donation to Scotland's Gardens Scheme

---

21. KILDALLOIG, Campbeltown ♿ (partially)

(Mr & Mrs Joe Turner)
Coastal garden with some interesting and unusual shrubs and herbaceous perennials. Woodland walk. Pond area under construction. Dogs on lead please.
Route: A83 to Campbeltown, then 3 miles south east of town past Davaar Island.
Admission £2.00 Accompanied children free.
OPEN BY APPOINTMENT. Tel: 01586 553192.
40% to Royal National Lifeboat Institution 60% net to Scotland's Gardens Scheme

---

22. KINLOCHLAICH HOUSE GARDENS, Appin ♿ (Gravel paths sloping)

(Mr & Mrs D E Hutchison & Miss F M M Hutchison)
Walled garden, incorporating the West Highlands' largest Nursery Garden Centre. Garden with beds of alpines, heathers, primulas, shrubs, rhododendrons, azaleas and herbaceous plants. Fruiting and flowering shrubs and trees. Woodland walk. Spring garden. Route: A828. Oban 18 miles, Fort William 27 miles. Bus stops at gate by Police Station.
Donation
OPEN ALL YEAR 9.30am - 5.30pm or dusk except Sundays October - March
(Sundays April - September 10.30am - 5.30pm) Closed Christmas & New Year. Except by appt.
40% to Appin Village Hall 60% net to SGS Charities

---

23. STRACHUR HOUSE FLOWER & WOODLAND GARDENS ♿

(Sir Charles & Lady Maclean)
Directly behind Strachur House, the flower garden is sheltered by magnificent beeches, limes, ancient yews and Japanese maples. There are herbaceous borders, a burnside rhododendron and azalea walk and a rockery. Old fashioned and species roses, lilies, tulips, spring bulbs and Himalayan poppies make a varied display in this informal haven of beauty and tranquillity. The garden gives onto Strachur Park, laid out by General Campbell in 1782, which offers spectacular walks through natural woodlands with 200-year-old trees, rare shrubs and a lochan rich in native wildlife. Teas. Plant stall. Route: turn off A815 at Strachur House Farm entrance; park in farm square.
Admission £2.50 Children 50p
FLOWER GARDEN OPEN SATURDAYS & SUNDAYS:
29 & 30 APRIL, 27 & 28 MAY, 1 & 2 JULY 1 - 5pm
40% to CLASP 60% net to SGS Charities

---

24. TOROSAY CASTLE & GARDENS, Isle of Mull

(Mr Christopher James)
Torosay is a beautiful and welcoming family home completed in 1858 by David Bryce in the Scottish Baronial style and is surrounded by 12 acres of spectacular contrasting gardens which include formal terraces and an impressive Italian statue walk, surrounded by informal woodland and water gardens. Many rare and tender plants. Tearoom. Gift shop. Adventure playground. Free parking. Groups welcome. 1½ miles from Craignure, A849 south. Miniature rail steam/ diesel from Craignure. Regular daily ferry service from Oban to Craignure.
Admission to Castle & Gardens £5.50 Children £2.25 Concessions £5.00
Castle open 1 May - 31 October. 10.30am - 5.00pm
GARDENS OPEN ALL YEAR
with reduced admission when Castle closed
Donation to Scotland's Gardens Scheme

AYRSHIRE

Joint District Organisers: **Mrs R F Cuninghame,** Caprington Castle, Kilmarnock KA2 9AA
                               Mrs John Greenall, Lagg House, Dunure KA7 4LE

Area Organisers: **Mrs Michael Findlay**, Carnell, Hurlford, Kilmarnock KA1 5JS
                     Mrs R Lewis, St. John's Cottage, Maybole KA19 7LN
                     Mrs John Mackay, Pierhill, Annbank, Ayr KA6 5AW
                     Mrs R McIntyre, Sorn Castle, Mauchline KA5 6HR

Hon. Treasurer: **Mr Hywel Davies,**   Peatland, Gatehead, Kilmarnock KA2 9AN

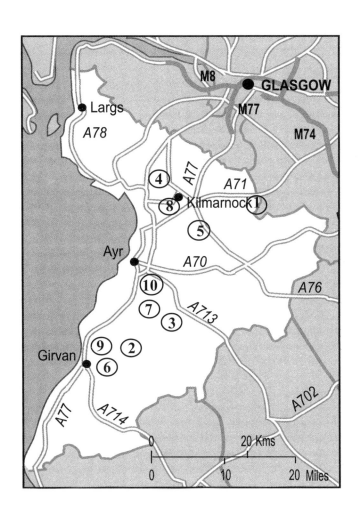

DATES OF OPENING

Blairquhan, Snowdrop & tree trail	Sunday 26 February	12 - 4pm
Borlandhills, Dunlop	Sunday 28 May	2 - 5pm
Avonhill Cottage, Drumclog....................................	Sunday 11 June	2 - 5pm
Peatland, Gatehead	Sunday 25 June	2 - 5pm
Ladyburn, By Maybole.	Sat 1 & Sun 2 July	2 - 5pm
Penkill Castle, near Girvan	Sunday 9 July	2 - 5pm
Barr Village Gardens.	Sat 15 & Sun 16 July	1 - 5pm
Carnell, Hurleford	Sunday 23 July	2 - 5pm
Skeldon, Dalrymple	Sunday 30 July	2 - 5pm
Glendoune, Girvan	Sunday 6 August	2 - 5pm

1. AVONHILL COTTAGE, Drumclog, Strathaven   ♿ (partly)
(Mr & Mrs E Chang)
A maturing garden of approximately 3.5 acres on an exposed site. The planting is varied and includes a woodland shelter belt and herbaceous plants, with 3 ponds and a bank of rhododendrons overlooking the river. Route: 5 miles from Strathaven on the A71 15 miles from Kilmarnock on A71 Drumclog Memorial Kirk turn onto B745 to Muirkirk. Avonhill is on right over hump back bridge. Teas. Plant Stall
Admission £3.00 Children free
SUNDAY 11 JUNE 2-5pm
40% to Cats Protection League   60% net to SGS Charities.

2. BARR VILLAGE GARDENS   ♿
A number of attractive gardens, some old, some new, within this small and beautiful conservation village. Teas in Barr Village Hall. Plant stall. Maps and tickets available outside Village Hall. Barr is on B734; Girvan 8 miles, Ballantrae 17 miles, Ayr 24 miles
Admission £3.00 Children free
SATURDAY & SUNDAY 15 & 16 JULY 1 - 5pm
40% to Childrens Hospice Association Scotland 60% net to SGS Charities

3. BLAIRQUHAN, Straiton, Maybole   ♿
(Mr & Mrs Patrick Hunter Blair)
Regency Castle built by William Burn, 1821 - 1842 for Sir David Hunter Blair 3rd Bart. Sixty-foot high saloon with gallery. The kitchen courtyard is formed with stones and sculpture from an earlier castle. All the original furniture for the house is still in it, there is a good collection of pictures and a gallery of paintings by the Scottish Colourists. 3 mile private drive along the River Girvan. Walled garden, pinetum and Regency glasshouse. The Castle is surrounded by an extensive park including an arboretum. There is a tree trail and a shop. Admission price includes a tour of the house. Tea in house. Near Kirkmichael, follow AA signs. Entry from B7045 over bridge half mile south of Kirkmichael.
Admission £6.00 Children £3.00 OAPs £4.00
SNOWDROP AND TREE TRAIL SUNDAY 26 FEBUARY 12 - 4pm
40% to Ayrshire Rivers Trust 60% net to SGS Charities

4. BORLANDHILLS, Dunlop ♿ (partly)

(Professor & Mrs Michael Moss)
This is a young hilltop garden, with magnificent views of Arran, created over the last nine years. It combines a surprising variety of habitats from a bog garden with gunnera, primula and great clumps of irises to dry sheltered corners with fine displays of bulbs in late spring, rhododendrons, azaleas and meconopsis. Roses and clematis scramble through hedges and over the buildings. There are large herbaceous borders, with many unusual Himalayan plants grown mostly from seed. In the heart of the garden are large vegetable plots that provide for the family throughout the year.
Route: From the centre of Dunlop down Main Street, turn left at the Church into Brecknabraes Road (right is the B706 to Beith) and garden is .7m on the left on the roadside. Teas and Plant Stall.
Admission £3.00 Children free
SUNDAY 28 MAY 2 - 5pm
40% between Dunlop Village Hall and Send a Cow 60% net to SGS Charities

---

5. CARNELL, Hurlford ♿

(Mr & Mrs J R Findlay & Mr & Mrs Michael Findlay)
Alterations in 1843 by William Burn. 16th century Peel Tower. 5 acres of gardens and lanscaped grounds and 100 metre phlox and shrub border. Extensive and spectacular herbaceous borders around Carnell House. Plant sale. Silver band. Ice cream and cream teas. Cars free. From A77 (Glasgow / Kilmarnock) take A76 (Mauchline / Dumfries) then right on to the A719 to Ayr for 1½ miles.
Admission £3.00 School children free. Special display by the Scottish Delphinium Society.
SUNDAY 23 JULY 2 - 5pm
40% between Craigie Parish Church & Craigie Village Hall and British Red Cross Society & Cancer Research 60% net to SGS Charities

---

6. GLENDOUNE, Girvan ♿ (partly)

(Major J C K Young)
The policies around the house contain rhododendrons, azaleas and fine specimen trees. The walled garden is currently in the process of reconstruction with herbaceous borders, bulbs, shrubs, fruit and vegetables. Route: A77 to Girvan - turn off at Shallochpark roundabout (½ mile). Teas and plant stall.
Admission £3.00 Children under 12 free.
SUNDAY 6 AUGUST 2 - 5pm
40% to Gurkha Welfare Trust 60% net to SGS Charities

✦ 7. LADYBURN, By Maybole ♿

(Mr and Mrs David Hepburn)
This old garden has been extensively re-designed and re-planted. Features include a burnside walk, herbaceous and shrub borders and a pond with marginal plantings. The garden now holds four national collections of roses whilst four further collections are currently being established. Plant stall. Teas. Route: Off B7023 /B741 Maybole / Crosshill / Dailly road signposted to 'Campsite'.
Admission £3.50 Children 50p *(No dogs please - except guide dogs)*
SATURDAY and SUNDAY 1 & 2 JULY 2 - 5pm
40% between Hope & Homes for children and Mental Health Foundation 60% net to SGS Charities

---

8. PEATLAND, Gatehead ♿

(Hywel & Tricia Davies)

This garden started from a green-field site 18 years ago and is an interesting example of what can be done in a fairly difficult climate. It contains a wide range of plants but the rhododendrons and roses are of special note. The roses are all large shrub roses grown within herbaceous borders. It is very much a country garden with an orchard and vegetable garden forming part of the interest for visitors. Route: Follow the A759 from Gatehead towards Troon and take the B751 towards Symington. Peatland lies a short way along on the right-hand side. Plants for sale. Teas available.

Admission £3.00 Children free

SUNDAY 25 JUNE 2 - 5pm

40% to Ayrshire & Arran Order of St. John 60% net to SGS Charities

---

9. PENKILL CASTLE, near Girvan ♿ (limited)

(Mr & Mrs Patrick Dromgoole)

A series of three Victorian gardens, one formal, one landscaped and one originally for vegetables, linked together by a 'wild walk' overlooking a burn leading to the Penwhapple River. Teas. Plant and other stalls, bagpipes and Scottish dancing. Route: 3 miles east of Girvan on Old Dailly to Barr road, B734.

Admission £3.00   School children free

SUNDAY 9 JULY 2 - 5pm

40% to Barr Parish Church 60% net to SGS Charities

---

10. SKELDON, Dalrymple

(Mr S E Brodie QC)

One and a half acres of formal garden with herbaceous borders and arched pathways. Large Victorian glasshouse with a substantial collection of plants. Four acres of woodland garden within a unique setting on the banks of the River Doon. Home baked teas. Silver band on the lawn. Plants stall. Route: From Dalrymple take B7034 Dalrymple/Hollybush road.

Admission £3.00 School children free

SUNDAY 30 JULY 2 - 5pm

40% to Princess Royal Trust for Carers 60% net to SGS Charities

---

National Council for the Conservation of Plants and Gardens

There are 7 National Collections in Ayrshire and Arran

NCCPG

1. 3 Groups of Hydrangea   2. Leucanthemum   3. Papaver orientale
4. 3 Groups of Rhododendron   5. Sambucus   6. Trillium
7. Rugosas. Pimpinellfolias (Scotch Roses). Portlands, climbing roses 1880 -1939

Visit their web site *www.nccpg.com* or call local information 01292 441430

The National Plant Collection Scheme©

BERWICKSHIRE

District Organiser:	**Mrs F Wills**, Anton's Hill, Coldstream TD12 4JD
Area Organisers:	**Mrs C Bailey,** Summerhill, Beauburn, Ayton TD14 5QY
	Miss Anthea Montgomery, Crooks Cottage, Hirsel, Coldstream TD12 4LR
Hon. Treasurer:	**Col S J Furness,** The Garden House, Netherbyres, Eyemouth TD14 5SE

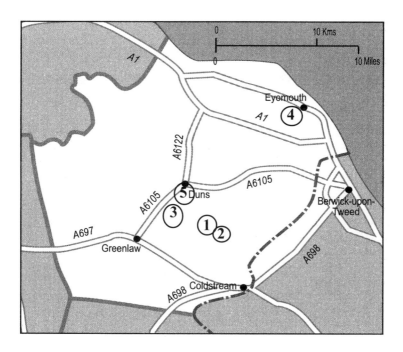

DATES OF OPENING

Bughtrig, Leitholm .... Open Daily 1 June-1 Sept   11am-5pm

Netherbyres, Eyemouth .... Sunday 9 April	2 - 5.30pm
Charterhall, Duns .... Sunday 14 May	12 - 5pm
Whitchester House, Berwickshire .... Sunday 28 May	2 - 5.30pm
Antons Hill, Leitholm .... Sunday 2 July	2 - 6pm
Netherbyres, Eyemouth .... Sunday 16 July	2 - 5.30pm

1. ANTONS HILL, Leitholm &

(Mr & Mrs Wills, Alec West & Pat Watson)
Well treed mature garden which has been improved and added to since 1999. There are woodland walks including a stumpery and large well planted pond, shrubberies and herbaceous borders together with a restored organic walled garden and greenhouse with a pear and apple orchard. Teas. Large Plant stall. Free rides on model railway. Route: Signed off B6461 west of Leitholm.
Admission £3.00 Children under 16 free
SUNDAY 2 JULY 2 - 6pm
40% to Oakfield (East Maudit) Ltd (Home for people with special needs) 60% net to SGS Charities

---

2. BUGHTRIG, Near Leitholm, Coldstream & (mainly)

(Major General & The Hon Mrs Charles Ramsay)
A traditional, hedged Scottish family garden, with an interesting combination of herbaceous plants, shrubs, annuals and fruit. It is surrounded by fine specimen trees which provide remarkable shelter. Small picnic area. Parking. Special arrangements, to include house visit, possible for bona fide groups. Accommodation in house possible for 4–6 guests. Half mile east of Leitholm on B6461.
Admission £2.00 Children under 18 £1.00
OPEN DAILY 1 JUNE TO 1 SEPTEMBER 11am - 5pm Contact tel: 01890 840678
Donation to Scotland's Gardens Scheme

---

3. CHARTERHALL, DUNS &

(Major & Mrs A Trotter)
Mature rhododendrons and azaleas in a woodland garden surounding a lovely family home with an outstanding view. Flower garden of roses, bulbs and perennial plants. Walled garden with newly designed vegetable garden and new greenhouse, which includes a small orchid house. Plant and Cake Stalls. Drawing (adult and children) - competitions and Plant naming competitions. Tombola. **LUNCH BBQ/SOUP AND ROLL 12-2pm. Teas 2.30-5pm.**
Route: 6 miles south-west of Duns, 3 miles east of Greenlaw, B6460.
Admission Adults £3.00 Children £1.00
SUNDAY 14 MAY 12 - 5pm
40% to Fogo Nursery School 60% net to SGS Charities

---

4. NETHERBYRES, Eyemouth

(Col S J Furness & Perennial (GRBS))
A unique 18th century elliptical walled garden. Daffodils and wild flowers in the spring. Annuals, roses, herbaceous borders, fruit and vegetables in the summer. Produce stall. Teas in house. ¼ mile south of Eyemouth on A1107 to Berwick.
Admission £3.00 Concessions £1.50
SUNDAY 9 APRIL 2 - 5.30pm
40% to EGunsgreen House Trust 60% net to SGS Charities
SUNDAY 16 JULY 2 - 5.30pm
Admission to garden £3.00 Concessions £1.50
40% to Perennial (GRBS) 60% net to SGS Charities
Parties of 10 or more by appointment at any time Tel: 018907 50337

---

5. WHITCHESTER HOUSE, Duns ♿ (partly)
(Teen Challenge)
A once famous rhododendron garden, now being brought back to life by young amateur gardeners, resident in the house. The lost garden of Berwickshire! Teas. Route B6355 Duns to Gifford Road, turn off at Ellemford.
Admission £3.00 Concessions £2.00 Children free
Sunday 28 May 2 - 5.30pm
40% to Teen Challenge   60% net to Scotland's Gardens Scheme

CAITHNESS & SUTHERLAND

District Organiser: **Mrs Judith Middlemas,** 22 Miller Place, Scrabster, Thurso, Caithness. KW14 7UH

Area Organiser: **Mrs Jonny Shaw,** Amat, Ardgay, Sutherland IV24 3BS

Hon. Treasurer: **Captain Colin Farley-Sutton**, **RN DL** Shepherd's Cottage, Watten, Caithness KW1 5UP

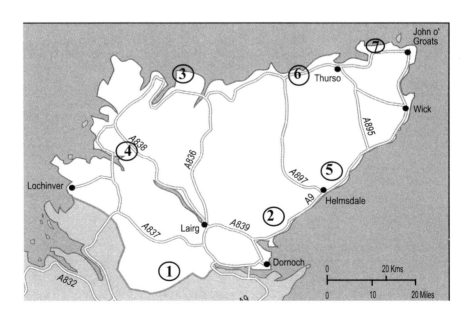

DATES OF OPENING

Kerrachar, Kylesku .... Mid May - mid Sept Tues, Thurs & Suns & By Appt.
Langwell, Berriedale .... By appointment

Amat, Ardgay	Sat & Sun 10 & 11 June	2- 5.00pm
Dunrobin Castle, Golspie	Saturday 1 July	10.30am - 5.30pm
The Castle & Gardens of Mey, Caithness	Wednesday 12 July	10.30am - 4pm
The Castle & Gardens of Mey, Caithness	Thursday 20 July	10.30am - 4pm
House of Tongue, Tongue	Saturday 29July	2 - 6pm
Sandside House, Reay	Sunday 30 July	2 - 5pm
Langwell, Berriedale	Sunday 6 August	2 - 5pm
Langwell, Berriedale	Sunday 13 August	2 - 5pm
The Castle & Gardens of Mey, Caithness	Saturday 19 August	10.30am - 4pm

1. AMAT, Ardgay   &&   (partially)
(Jonny and Sara Shaw)
For twenty years the garden has been mainly forgotten and a new garden is now being created
using the old one as a guideline. Woodland and a river walk. Take road from Ardgay to Croick.
Admission £3.00 Children 50p
SATURDAY & SUNDAY 10 &11 JUNE 2 - 5.00pm
40% between Croick Church & Help The Aged 60% net to SGS Charities

2. DUNROBIN CASTLE & GARDENS, Golspie
(The Sutherland Trust)
Formal gardens laid out in 1850 by the architect, Barry. Set beneath the fairytale castle of
Dunrobin. Tearoom and gift shop in castle. Picnic site and woodland walks. Dunrobin Castle
Museum in the gardens. Suitable for disabled by prior arrangement. Stunning falconry display.
(Group admission: Adults £5.60, children & OAPs £4.50, family £17.50.)
Castle one mile north of Golspie on A9.
Admission £6.60 Children £4.50 OAPs £5.70
SATURDAY 1 JULY 10.30am - 5.30pm (Last admission 5pm)
40% to Imperial Cancer Research Fund 60% net to SGS Charities

3. HOUSE OF TONGUE, Tongue, Lairg   &&   (partially)
(The Countess of Sutherland)
17th century house on Kyle of Tongue. Walled garden, herbaceous borders, old fashioned roses.
Teas. Tongue half a mile. House just off main road approaching causeway.
Admission to garden £2.50 OAPs £2.00 Children 50p
SATURDAY 29 JULY 2 - 6pm
40% to Children 1st 60% net to SGS Charities

4. KERRACHAR, Kylesku
(Peter & Trisha Kohn)
Plantsman's garden and small nursery begun in 1995, beautifully located in an extremely remote and wild coastal setting. Wide range of hardy perennials and shrubs. Featured in "The Garden" and "The English Garden" in 2002. Access only by 25 minute boat journey from Kylesku (£10). Garden admission £2.50 Children under 12 free Under 16 half price. (boat and garden)
OPEN mid MAY - mid SEPTEMBER Tuesdays, Thursdays and Sundays
All sailings at 13.00 from Kylesku (Old Ferry Pier)
Additional visits for groups by arrangement. Tel: 01571 833288 email:

---

5. LANGWELL, Berriedale &
(The Lady Anne Bentinck)
A beautiful old walled-in garden situated in the secluded Langwell strath. Charming access drive with a chance to see deer. Cars free. Teas served under cover. Plants for sale. Berriedale 2 miles. Route A9.
Admission £3.00 Children under 12 free OAPs £2.50
SUNDAYS 6 & 13 AUGUST 2 - 5pm
Also by appointment. Tel: 01593 751278
40% to RNLI 60% net to SGS Charities

---

6. SANDSIDE HOUSE GARDENS by Reay, Thurso & (partially)
(Mr & Mrs Geoffrey Minter)
Old walled gardens restored and well stocked. Sunken rectangular walled garden. Upper garden with sea views to the Orkneys and Grade A listed 2-seater privy. Terrace with rockery overlooking sunken garden. Main gate is on A836 half mile west of Reay village. Teas. Plant stall. There is a splayed entrance with railings and gate lodge.
Admission £3.00 OAPs £2.00 children 50p
SUNDAY 30 JULY 2 - 5pm
40% to Reay and District Garden Club 60% net to SGS Charities

---

7. THE CASTLE & GARDENS OF MEY, Caithness &
(The Queen Elizabeth Castle of Mey Trust)
Originally a Z plan castle bought by the Queen Mother in 1952 and then restored and improved. The walled garden and the East Garden were also created by the Queen Mother. Teas served in Old Granary. Route on A836 between Thurso and John O'Groats, 1½ miles from Mey.
Admission to Gardens only £3.00 Concession £2.50
Castle and Gardens: £7.00 Concessions £6.00 Children and cars free
WEDNESDAY 12 JULY 10.30am - 4.00pm
THURSDAY 20 JULY 10.30am - 4.00pm
SATURDAY 19 AUGUST 10.30am - 4.00pm
40% Queen's Nursing Institute (Scotland) 60% net to SGS Charities

---

Why not look up the gardens on our website?
www.gardensofscotland.org
PHOTOS AND MAPS

CLYDESDALE

Joint District Organisers: **Mr Charles Brandon,** Cherry Tree Cottage, 2 Glenburn Avenue, Symington ML12 6LH
Mrs M Maxwell Stuart, Baitlaws, Lamington ML12 6HR

Area Organiser: **Mrs Irene Miller,** West End, 4 Main Street, Carnwath ML11 8JZ
PR - **Mr G Crouch,** 113 High Street, Biggar ML12 6DL

Hon Treasurer: **Mrs Edna Munro,** High Meadows, Nemphlar, Lanark ML11 9JF

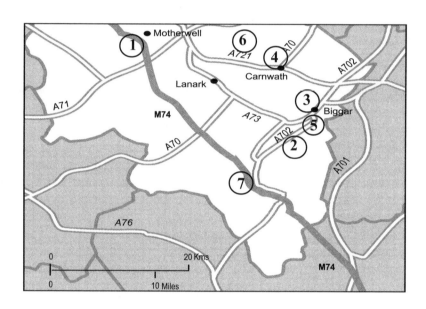

DATES OF OPENING

Baitlaws, Lamington .... By appointment June, July, August
Biggar Park, Biggar.. By appointment Groups May - July

Biggar Park, Biggar..	Sunday 4 June	12am - 5pm
Dippoolbank Cottage, Carnwath	Sunday 18 June	2 - 6pm
Baitlaws, Lamington	Sunday 25 June	2 - 5pm
20 Smithycroft, Hamilton	Sunday 2 July	11am - 5pm
Drakelaw Pottery, Crawfordjohn	Sunday 2 July	2 - 5.30pm
Dippoolbank Cottage, Carnwath	Sunday 16 July	2 - 6pm
Carnwath Village Garden Trail, Carnwath	Sunday 23 July	1.30 - 6pm
Culter Allers, Coulter	Sunday 13 August	2 - 5pm

✿ 1. 20 SMITHYCROFT, Hamilton ♿

(Mr & Mrs R.I. Fionda)
A plantswoman's garden which has been developed over the past seven years. Eucalyptus, phormiums and clematis abound and there is a large range of unusual plants which only flourish in sheltered parts of Scotland. Teas. Plant Stall Route: off M74 at Junction 6. 1mile on A72, well signed.
Admission £3.00 Children free
SUNDAY 2 JULY 11am - 5pm
40% to Friends of Saint Mary (South African Clinic) 60% net to SGS Charities

---

2. BAITLAWS, Lamington, Biggar

(Mr & Mrs M Maxwell Stuart)
The garden is set at over 900ft above sea level and has been developed over the past twenty five years with a particular emphasis on colour combinations of shrubs and herbaceous perennials which flourish at that height. The surrounding hills make an imposing backdrop. Opening again in June this year to enable visitors to fill gaps in their own borders. Large plant stall. Teas. Route: off A702 above Lamington village. Biggar 5 miles, Abington 5 miles, Lanark 10 miles.
Admission £3.00 Children under 12 free
SUNDAY 25 JUNE 2 - 5pm
By Appointment JUNE, JULY & AUGUST Tel: 01899 850240
40% to Biggar Museum Trust, Lamington Chapel Restoration Fund 60% net to SGS Charities

---

3. BIGGAR PARK, Biggar   ♿ (partially)

(Mr & Mrs David Barnes)
Ten acre garden, starred in 'Good Gardens Guide', featured on 'The Beechgrove Garden' and in 'Country Life'. Incorporating traditional working walled garden with long stretches of herbaceous borders, shrubberies, fruit, vegetables and greenhouses. Lawns, walks, pools, Japanese garden and other interesting features. Glades of rhododendrons, azaleas and blue poppies in May and June. Good collection of old fashioned and new species roses in July. Interesting young trees. On A702, quarter mile south of Biggar.
SUNDAY 4 JUNE noon - 5pm. GARDEN OPEN AND GRAND FETE, Teas, Stalls etc. including plant stall, in conjunction with the Biggar Rotary Club, entrance takings to Scotland's Gardens Scheme.
Admission £3.00
Groups welcome by appointment MAY - JULY. Tel: 01899 220185.

---

4. CARNWATH VILLAGE GARDEN TRAIL

Parking at car park at the top of the village on the A70 where the trail plan will be available, the trail through this conservation village commences from the Peebles road down the south side of the main street (A721) calling in at gardens on the way to the Jubilee Garden at St. Mary's Aisle. Returning by the north side visitors are invited to call in at the Church Hall for home made cream teas, coffee and plant stalls, eventually returning to the car park.   Route: A721 from Carluke and west, A70 'Lang Whang' from Edinburgh.
Admission £3.00 Children under 14 free
SUNDAY 23 JULY 1.30 - 6pm
40% between Carnwath Parish Church Restoration Fund and Carnwath Evergreen Club 60% net to SGS Charities

---

5. CULTER ALLERS, Coulter   ♿ (partially)

(The McCosh Family)

Culter Allers, a late-Victorian gothic house, has maintained its traditional one-acre walled kitchen garden. this has been developed into a decorative potager providing over 70 varieties of vegetables with fruit and cut flowers. Peas and sweet peas, black beans and beetroot, sweetcorn and snapdragons, are bordered by box hedges. There are herbaceous borders surrounding a lawn, annual borders and a well. The remainder of the grounds of the house are open and include a woodland walk, an avenue of 125 year old lime trees leading to the Village Church. Teas and a plant stall. In the village of Coulter, 3 miles south of Biggar on A702

Admission £3.00   Children free

SUNDAY 13 AUGUST 2 - 5pm

40% to Coulter Library Trust   60% net to SGS Charitie

---

6. DIPPOOLBANK COTTAGE, Carnwath

(Mr Allan Brash)

Artist's intriguing cottage garden. Vegetables grown in small beds. Herbs, fruit, flowers. Garden now extended to include pond, with flowers, trees, etc. Plant stall. Wooden toadstools. Tree house now completed. Teas in the lean to. Route: off B7016, 2½ miles Carnwath. Well signed.

Admission £3.00   Children free

SUNDAYS 18 JUNE & 16 JULY 2 - 6pm

40% to Cancer Relief Macmillan Fund   60% net to SGS Charitie

---

7. DRAKELAW POTTERY, Crawfordjohn

(Mark & Liz Steele)

The cottage once formed part of the grounds of Gilkerscleugh House and is now set in woodland and gardens created in the last thirteen years by a landscape architect and his family. The garden comprises imaginative combinations of perennial, shrub and tree planting surrounding a lawn, terrace, spring fed ponds and Garden Burn. There is an emphasis on bold and vigerous plants that are hardy despite the aspect and elevation of the garden. Teas, plants and a sale of decorative and functional pottery. Sorry no dogs. Route: Located on the road to Crawfordjohn 2½ miles from junction 13 on the M74 and 2 miles from the village.

Admission £3.00   Children free

SUNDAY 2 JULY 2 - 5.30pm

40% to The British Red Cross   60% net to SGS Charities

DUMFRIES

District Organiser	**Mrs Sarah Landale**, Dalswinton House, Auldgirth
Area Organisers:	**Mrs Fiona Bell-Irving** Bankside, Kettleholm, Lockerbie.
Hon. Treasurer:	**Mr J. Smith** Kirkmichael Old Manse, Parkgate, Dumfries DG1 3LY

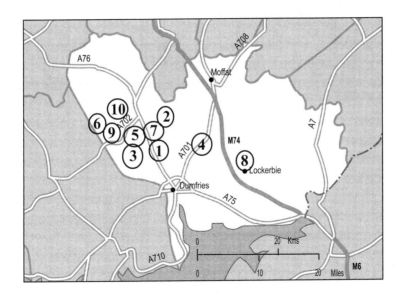

DATES OF OPENING

Dalswinton House, Auldgirth	Sunday 9 April	2 - 5pm
Portrack House, Holywood	Sunday 7 May	12 - 5pm
Dalswinton House, Auldgirth	Sunday 14 May	2 - 5pm
Peilton, Moniave (Joint)	Sunday 21 May	2 - 6pm
Townhead of Glencairn, Moniaive (Joint)	Sunday 21 May	2 - 6pm
Glenae, Amisfield	Sunday 4 June	2 - 5pm
Grovehill House, Burnhead	Sunday 11 June	2 - 5pm
Dunesslin, Dunscore	Sunday 18 June	2 - 5pm
The Garth, Tynron	Sunday 25 June	2 - 5pm
Ravenshill House Hotel, Lockerbie	Sunday 2 July	3 - 6pm
Cowhill Tower, Holywood	Sunday 16 July	2 - 5pm

1. COWHILL TOWER, Holywood
(Captain & Mrs A E Weatherall)
Splendid views from lawn down Nith Valley. Interesting walled garden. Topiary animals, birds and figures. Woodland walk. Produce stall. Teas under cover. Holywood 1½ miles off A76, 5 miles north of Dumfries.
Admission £3.00 Children £1.00
SUNDAY 16 July 2 - 5pm
40% to Macmillan Cancer Relief 60% net to SGS Charities

2. DALSWINTON HOUSE, Auldgirth
(Mr & Mrs Peter Landale)
In April daffodil walk along woodland and lochside. In May woodland and lochside walks. Cake stall. Home baked teas. Dumfries 7 miles. Dumfries/Auldgirth bus via Kirkton stops at lodge. Admission: £3.00 Children 50p
SUNDAYS 9 APRIL & 14 MAY 2 – 5pm
April opening - 40% to The Pituitary Foundation   *60% net to SGS Charities*
May opening - 40% to Kirkmahoe Parish Church   *60% net to SGS Charities*

❀ 3. DUNESSLIN, Dunscore
(Iain & Zara Milligan)
The garden is set in the hills with magnificent views. The centre piece is a walled garden containing varied shrubs, trees and herbacious plants. It leads by steps and terraces to a box-edged rose garden which in turn leads to a small enclosed garden beside the house. Nearby is a woodland garden which is currently being restored. Within half an hour walk from the house there are three fine cairns by Andy Goldsworthy. Route: take Corsock Road out of Dunscore, approximately 1½ miles right by telephone box to Corsock. First crossroads left.
Admission £3.00 Children 50p
SUNDAY 18 JUNE 2 - 5pm
40% net to Dunscore Church   60% net to SGS Charities

❀ 4. GLENAE, Amisfield ♿
(Mr & Mrs Sebastian Morley)
A beautiful walled garden with many borders well stocked with interesting plants. Teas. Plant Stall. Route: 1.5 miles north of Amisfield on A701. Turn right to Duncow/Auldgirth. 1 mile on right.
Admission £3.00 Children 50p
SUNDAY 4 JUNE 2 - 5pm
40% to SSAFA Forces Help 60% net to SGS Charities

---

5. GROVEHILL HOUSE, Burnhead, Thornhill
(Mr & Mrs Alan Paterson)
Two acre terraced garden on a precipitous site; planned and planted for year round interest. Route: One mile west of Thornhill on A702. Parking in field west of Burnhead Brae.
Teas available locally. Produce stall from Loch Arthur Community.
Admission £3.00 Children free
Teas available locally. Produce stall from Loch Arthur Community.
SUNDAY 11 JUNE 2 - 5pm
40% to The Loch Arthur Community, The Camphill Village Trust 60% net to SGS Charitie

---

6. PEILTON, Moniaive
(Muray & Alison Graham)
The 3½ acre landscaped woodland garden has been extensively planted up over the last 12 years. Mature nature trees are complemented with interesting ground cover, with exotic species and a natural burn. Teas. Route: Off A802 between Kirkland of Glencairn & Moniaive.
Joint Opening with Townhead of Glencairn - Admission: £4.00 Children 50p
SUNDAY 21 MAY 2 - 6pm
40% to RIED 60% net to SGS Charities

---

7. PORTRACK HOUSE, Holywood
(Charles Jencks)
Original 18th century manor house with Victorian addition; octagonal folly-library. Twisted, undulating landforms and terraces designed by Charles Jencks as 'The Garden of Cosmic Speculation'; lakes designed by Maggie Keswick; rhododendrons, large new greenhouse in a geometric Kitchen Garden of the Six Senses; Glengower Hill plantation and view; woodland walks with Nonsense Building (architect: James Stirling); Universe cascade and rail garden of the Scottish Worthies; interesting sculpture including that of DNA. Teas. Route: Holywood 1½ miles off A76, five miles north of Dumfries.
Admission £6.00
SUNDAY 7 MAY 12 - 5pm
40% to Maggie's Centre, Western General Hospital, Edinburgh   60% net to SGS Charities

---

✪ 8. RAVENSHILL HOUSE HOTEL, Lockerbie
(Norman & Sheila Tindal)
The Hotel, built in 1874, as the house for the Factor of the then Lockerbie Estate is set in 1.5 acres of mature gardens. Interesting collection of herbaceous plants; admirable vegetables and fruit in a walled garden for hotel use. Patio and pond area. Pretty, small Victorian greenhouse with a very old vine. Teas in garden and hotel conservatory. Plant Stall. Parking. Entrance off A709 Dumfries to Lockerbie road, just as you come into Lockerbie
Admission £3.00
SUNDAY 2 JULY 3 - 6pm
20% British Heart Foundation 20% Cancer Research 60% net to SGS Charities

---

9. THE GARTH, Tynron
(Mimi & Christopher Craig)
Old manse, established 1750 with additions. 2 acre garden, woodland, waterside and walled garden. Teas in Tynron Village Hall. Route: Off A702 between Penpont and Moniaive.
Admission £3.00 Children 50p
SUNDAY 25 JUNE 2 - 5pm
40% to Village Hall Fund 60% net to SGS Charities

---

10. TOWNHEAD OF GLENCAIRN, Kirkland, by Moniaive
(Annabel Stapleton & Robert Leighton)
The south-facing house sits on a hill protected by established trees. A burn has been diverted to run through the garden into a lochan surrounded by water loving plants. To the side of the house the beds are terraced and planted with Mediterranean plants. Perolas are adorned with old fashioned climbing roses and clematis. Plant stall - Refreshments. (Teas available at Peilton) Route: On A702 between Thornhill and Moniaive at Kirkland of Glencairn.
Joint Opening with Peilton - Admission: £4.00 Children 50p
SUNDAY 21 MAY 2 - 6pm
40% to Oncology Unit Fund - Dumfries and Galloway Royal Infirmary 60% net to SGS Charities

---

Why not look up the gardens on our website?
www.gardensofscotland.org
PHOTOS AND MAPS

DUNBARTONSHIRE WEST

District Organiser: **Mrs K Murray,** 7 The Birches, Shandon, Helensburgh G84 8HN

Area Organisers: **Mrs J Christie,** Gartlea, Gartocharn G83 9LX
                       Mrs R Lang, Ardchapel, Shandon, Helensburgh G84 8NP
                       Mrs R Macaulay, Denehard, Garelochhead G84 0EL
                       Mrs J Theaker, 19 Blackhill Drive, Helensburgh G84 9AF

Hon. Treasurer: **Mrs H Wands,** Lindowan, Rhu G84 8NH

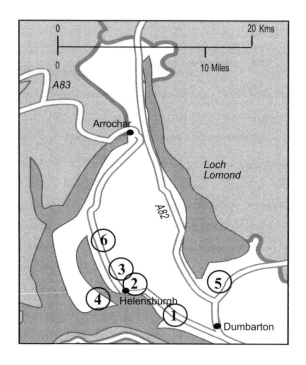

DATES OF OPENING

Glenarn, Rhu .... Daily 21 March - 21 September   Sunrise - sunset

Kilarden, Rosneath	Sunday 23 April	2 - 5.30pm
Geilston Garden, Cardross	Sunday 14 May	1 - 5pm
Ross Priory, Gartocharn	Sunday 21 May	2 - 5.30pm
Shandon Gardens, Helensburgh	Sunday 28 May	2 - 5pm
Hill House Plant Sale, Helensburgh	Sunday 3 September	11am - 4pm

1. GEILSTON GARDEN, Cardross ♿

(The National Trust for Scotland)

The present design of Geilston Garden was laid out over 200 years ago to enhance Geilston House, which dates back to the late 17th century. The garden has many attractive features including the walled garden wherein a notable specimen of *Sequioadendron giganteum* dominates the lawn and the herbaceous border provides summer colour on a grand scale. In addition a wide range of fruit, vegetables and cut flowers is still cultivated in the kitchen garden. The Geilston Burn winds its way through enchanting woodland walks which provide spring displays of bluebells and azaleas. Tea and shortbread. Plant stall. Sorry, no dogs. Route A814, Cardross 1 mile.

Admission £3.00 Children under 12 free

SUNDAY 14 MAY 1 - 5pm

40% to The Gardens Fund of The National Trust for Scotland   60% net to SGS Charities

2. GLENARN, Rhu, Dunbartonshire

(Michael & Sue Thornley and family)

Sheltered woodland garden overlooking the Gareloch, famous for its collection of rare and tender rhododendrons, together with fine magnolias and other interesting trees and shrubs. Beneath are snowdrops, crocus, daffodils, erythroniums and primulas in abundance. Work still continues in the rock garden (a long project) and there are beehives near the vegetable patch. Collection box, dogs on leads please and cars to be left at gate unless passengers are infirm. On A814, two miles north of Helensburgh.

Minimum donation £3.00 Children and concessions £1.50

DAILY 21 MARCH - 21 SEPTEMBER Sunrise - sunset

Donation to Scotland's Gardens Scheme

3. HILL HOUSE, Helensburgh   ♿ (garden only)

(The National Trust for Scotland)

SCOTLAND'S GARDENS SCHEME PLANT SALE is held in the garden of The Hill House, which has fine views over the Clyde estuary and is considered Charles Rennie Mackintosh's domestic masterpiece. The gardens continue to be restored to the patron's planting scheme with many features that reflect Mackintosh's design.

Admission to Plant Sale free. No dogs please. Donations to SGS welcome

(The Hill House tea room open from 11am.) House open separately 1.30 - 5.30pm.

Admission may be restricted and usual charges apply.

SUNDAY 3 SEPTEMBER 11am - 4pm

40% to The Gardens Fund of the National Trust for Scotland   60% net to SGS Charities

4. KILARDEN, Rosneath, Dumbartonshire

(Mr & Mrs J. E. Rowe)

Sheltered, hilly 10 acre woodland with notable collection of species and hybrid rhododendrons collected over a period of 50 years by the late Neil and Joyce Rutherford. Paths may be muddy. Not suitable for wheelchairs. Dogs on leads please. Plant stall. Teas in Church Hall in village. Route: ¼ mile from Rosneath off B833 .

Admission to Garden £1.50   Children free

SUNDAY 23 APRIL 2 - 5.30pm

40% to Friends of St Modan's, Rosneath   60% net to SGS Charities

5. ROSS PRIORY Gartocharn ♿
(University of Strathclyde)
1812 Gothic addition by James Gillespie Graham to house of 1693 overlooking Loch Lomond.
Rhododendrons, azaleas, selected shrubs and trees. Walled garden with glasshouses, pergola,
ornamental plantings. Family burial ground. Nature and garden trails. Putting Green. Plant
stall. Tea in house. House not open to view. Cars free. Gartocharn 1½ miles off A811. Bus:
Balloch to Gartocharn leaves Balloch at 1 pm and 3 pm.
Admission £2.00 Children free
SUNDAY 21 MAY 2 - 5.30pm
40% to CHAS 60% net to SGS Charities

6. SHANDON GARDENS, Helensburgh
Ardchapel   (Mr & Mrs J S Lang)
Ardchapel Lodge   (Mr & Mrs C E Hudson)
The Birches   (Mr & Mrs R Murray)
Interesting combination of gardens overlooking the Gareloch, about five acres in all.
Rhododendrons, azaleas and other shrubs and trees. Wooded area with burn and bank of
bluebells. Well planned cottage garden and a small intensively planted garden in The Birches.
Cup of tea and shortbread. Plant stall. Baking stall. Sorry no dogs 3¾ miles north west of
Helensburgh on A814. Parking on service road below houses.
Admission £3.00 includes all gardens. Children under 12 free.
SUNDAY 28 MAY 2 - 5pm
40% to Sight Savers 60% net to SGS Charities

EAST LOTHIAN

District Organiser: **Mrs Max Ward,** Stobshiel House, Humbie EH36 5PD
                                     Tel: 01875 833646

Area Organisers: **Mrs S M Edington,** Meadowside Cottage, Strathearn Road,
                                     North Berwick EH39 5BZ
                                     Mrs C Gwyn, The Walled Garden, Tyninghame,
                                     Dunbar EH42 1XW
                                     Mrs W M C Kennedy, Oak Lodge, Inveresk,
                                     Musselburgh EH21 7TE
                                     Mrs N Parker, Steading Cottage, Stevenson, Haddington EH41 4PU
                                     Mrs J Campbell Reid, Sylvan Cottage, Goose Green Road,
                                     Gullane EH31 2AT

Hon. Treasurer: **Mr S M Edington,** Meadowside Cottage, Strathearn Road,
                                     North Berwick EH39 5BZ

DATES OF OPENING
Inwood, Carberry .... See website: www.inwoodgarden.com
                                                                        for details of other opening times.
Shepherd House, Inveresk .... Tues & Thurs 2 - 4pm Apr, May & June
                                                                        & By appointment Tel: 0131 665 2570
Stobshiel House, Humbie .... By appointment Tel: 01875 833646
                                                                        email: wardhersey@aol.com

Torosay Castle and Gardens, Isle of Mull
Gardens open all year
Photographer: Angela Jayne Barnett

Wemyss Castle, East Wemyss
Sunday 9th April 2-5pm

Photographer: Ray Cox

Gorno Grove House, by Strathmiglo
Sunday 28th May 2-5.30pm

Photographer: Ray Cox

Gallery, Montrose
Sunday 9th July 2-5pm

Photographer: Ray Cox

St Monans, small gardens
Sunday 4th June 2-5pm

Old Sun Inn, Newbattle
By appointment (most days) 1st May–30th July
Photographer: Brenda White

Barrondale House, Newbattle
Saturday 8th & Sunday 9th July 2–5pm
Photographer: Brenda White

Haystoun, Peebles
Sunday 28th May 1.30–5.30pm
Photographer: Brenda White

Attadale, Strathcarron
1st April–end October 10.30am–5.30pm closed Sundays
Saturday 3rd June 2-5pm

Armaddy Castle, Balvicar, by Oban
Daily all year 9am-sunset

Antons Hill, Leitholm
Sunday 2nd July 2-6pm

Ardchattan Priory, North Connel
Daily from 1st April-31st October 9am-6pm
A fete will be held on Sunday 30th July noon-4pm

Earlshall Castle, Leuchars
Sunday 25th June 2-5pm
Sunday 16th July 2-5pm

Edzell Village
Sunday 2nd July 2-5pm

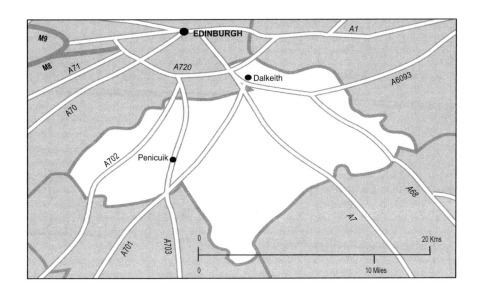

Winton House, Pencaitland	Sunday 2 April	12.30 - 4.30pm
Shepherd House, Inveresk	Sunday 30 April	2 - 5pm
Shepherd House, Inveresk	Sunday 14 May	2 - 5pm
Tyninghame House, Dunbar	Sunday 14 May	1 - 5pm
Stobshiel, Humbie	Sunday 21 May	2 - 5pm
Inwood, Carberry	Sunday 28 May	2 - 5.30pm
Stenton Village Gardens	Sunday 4 June	2 - 5pm
Greywalls, Gullane	Saturday 10 June	2 - 5pm
Inveresk, Near Musselburgh	Sat & Sun 10 & 11 June	2 - 5pm
Shepherd House, Inveresk	Sat & Sun 10 & 11 June	2 - 5pm
Dirleton Village.	Sat & Sun 17 & 18 June	2 - 5pm
Blackdykes, North Berwick	Sunday 18 June	2 - 5pm
Tyninghame House, Dunbar	Sunday 25 June	1 - 5pm
Gifford Village Gardens, North Berwick	Sunday 2 July	2 - 6pm
Gateside House, Gullane	Sunday 9 July	2 - 5pm
SGS 10th Anniversary Plant Sale, Dalkeith	Saturday 14 October	9am - 2.30pm

❀ **1. BLACKDYKES, North Berwick**
(Hew & Janey Dalrymple)
Created from farmland over the past twelve years. Blackdykes has a semi-formal walled garden with herbaceous borders and Irish yew avenue, a formal box-edged parterre with large collection of old roses, shrub walk, horn beam hedges, newley planted and yew alleé and potager. Teas. Plants. Route: Right turn off A198 North Berwick to Dunbar Road. 2 miles from centre of North Berwick.
Admission £3.00   Children under 12 free
SUNDAY 18 JUNE 2 - 5pm
40% to Help the Aged   60% net to SGS Charities

65

2. DIRLETON VILLAGE   ♿

Dirleton is a beautiful conservation village with a large green, a historic church and a castle. Gardens of various sizes and types are open throughout the village. Parking, tickets and maps are available at the green. Teas are served in the church hall. Also this year, there is a flower festival in the church.

Admission £3.00, children free, to all open gardens.

SATURDAY & SUNDAY 17 & 18 JUNE 2 - 5pm

40% to Oxfam 60% net to SGS Charities

---

3. GATESIDE HOUSE, Gullane

(Mr F Kirwan)

This is a mature one acre garden by the sea, planted for year-round interest with shrubaceous borders, perennial grasses, annual planting, vegetable garden, orchard, fruit cage and large greenhouse. Large number of agapanthus, delphiniums, chrysanthemums and pelargoniums. Route: Plant stall. Follow signs for the beach in Gullane, Whim Road is the first turn on the left. Gateside House is the fourth entrance on the right.

Admission £3.00

SUNDAY 9 JULY 2 - 5pm

40% to Oxfam 60% net to SGS Charities

---

4. GIFFORD VILLAGE GARDENS, Gifford   ♿ (some)

Gifford is an attractive conservation village. Various gardens, small and large, in and around the village will be open. Teas. Plant stall. Tickets and maps available from several village and garden locations. Route: follow B6369 from Haddington or B6355 from Tranent/Pencaitland.

Admission £3.50 Children free

SUNDAY 2 JULY 2 - 6pm

40% to Gifford Horticultural Society 60% net to SGS Charities

---

5. GREYWALLS HOTEL, Gullane

(Mr & Mrs Giles Weaver)

Six acres of formal garden attributed to Gertrude Jekyll complements the Edwardian house built by Sir Edwin Lutyens in 1901. Formal garden, herbaceous, shrub and annual borders. Teas and Plant Stall.

Admission £3.00 Accompanied children free

SATURDAY 10 JUNE 2 - 5pm

All takings to Scotland's Gardens Scheme

6. INVERESK, Near Musselburgh

This year you have the exciting prospect of visiting at least seven of the inspirational and constantly changing walled gardens of Inveresk, a chance which comes one weekend in two years. Each garden has its own individual character and personality displaying a wide variety of interesting and unusual trees, shrubs and plants. They will include Catherine Lodge, Eskhill, Inveresk Lodge, The Manor House, Oak Lodge, Rose Court and Shepherd House. Inveresk, standing on a ridge to the south of Musselburgh, is an elegant and historic village. Although there have been settlements since Roman times the present houses mostly date from the late 17th and early 18th centuries. The sounds of lawn-mowing and hedge-cutting will be heard all over the village in the weeks preceding our open week-end, when we look forward to giving you a warm welcome and a home-baked tea, whatever the weather! St. Michael's Kirk will be open to the public on both days from 2-4pm. Plant stalls. Teas.
Admission includes all open gardens £4.50 Children free.
SATURDAY & SUNDAY 10 & 11 JUNE 2 - 5pm
40% to The Scottish Association for Children with Heart Disorders 60% net to SGS Charities

---

7. INWOOD, Carberry   ♿ (with help)

(Mr & Mrs Irvine Morrison)
Approached through an avenue of towering Scots pines and English oaks, Inwood is a place of surprise and delight. Created from scratch over 20 years, the generously proportioned island beds teem with carefully considered combinations of plants and colours that can easily be translated into smaller gardens. Adventurous planting reaches a peak in high summer when 40% shrubs, herbaceous perennials, cascading clematis and billowing roses provide glorious bursts of colour and hints of sweet perfumes. 2 greenhouses with begonia and streptocarpus collections. Pond. Teas and plant stall. No dogs please. Route: 1 mile south of Whitecraig on A6124. RHS partnership garden.
Admission £3.00 Accompanied children free
SUNDAY 28 MAY 2 - 5.30pm
All takings to Scotland's Gardens Scheme
*Garden open at other times see website:***www.inwoodgarden.com** *Email:* **lindsay@inwoodgarden.com**

---

8. SHEPHERD HOUSE, Inveresk, near Musselburgh

(Sir Charles & Lady Fraser)
Shepherd House and its one-acre garden form a walled triangle in the middle of the 18th century village of Inveresk. The main garden is to the rear of the house, where the formality of the front garden is continued with a herb parterre and two symmetrical potagers. A formal rill runs the length of the garden, beneath a series of rose, clematis and wistaria pergolas and arches, and connects the two ponds. The formality is balanced by the romance of the planting. Ann Fraser is an artist and the garden provides much of her inspiration. There will be an Exhibition of her paintings in the garden gallery on all garden open days from 20th April till 30th June.
Admission £2.50 Children free
SUNDAYS 30 APRIL & 14 MAY 2 - 5pm
SATURDAY & SUNDAY 10 & 11 JUNE 2 - 5pm (see Inveresk entry)
GARDEN ALSO OPEN TUESDAY & THURSDAY 2-4pm in APRIL, MAY & JUNE
Groups welcome by appointment Telephone 0131 665 2570
Email ann@fraser2570.freeserve.co.uk Web site www.shepherdhousegarden.co.uk
40% to The National Art Collections Fund 60% net to SGS Charities

---

9. STENTON VILLAGE GARDENS

Stenton is a lovely conservation village at the edge of the Lammermuir hills, with a great variety of gardens, large and small, old and new in an around the village. Tickets, maps and teas available in the village hall on the green. Plant stall. Follow signs from A199 East Linton/ Dunbar.
Admission £3.50
SUNDAY 4 JUNE 2 – 5pm
40% to Richard Cave MS Holiday Centre 60% net to SGS Charities

---

10. STOBSHIEL HOUSE, Humbie

(Mr & Mrs Maxwell Ward)
A large garden to see for all seasons. Walled garden adjacent to the house, box-edged borders filled with herbaceous plants, bulbs, roses and lavendar beds. Rustic summerhouse. Glasshouse. Shrubbery with rhododendrons, azaleas and bulbs. Water garden with meconopsis and primulas. Formal lily pond. Woodland walks. Home made teas. Plant stall. Route: B6368 Haddington/Humbie roadsign, Stobshiel 1 mile.
Admission £3.00 OAPs £2.00 Children under 12 free
SUNDAY 21 MAY 2 - 5pm
Open by appointment at other times Tel: 01875 833646 or Email:*wardhersey@aol.com*
40% to Cancer Research UK. 60% net to SGS Charities

---

11. TYNINGHAME HOUSE, Dunbar

(Tyninghame Gardens Ltd)
Splendid 17th century pink sandstone Scottish baronial house, remodelled in 1829 by William Burn, rises out of a sea of plants. Herbaceous border, formal rose garden, Lady Haddington's secret garden with old fashioned roses, formal walled garden with sculpture and yew hedges. The 'wilderness' spring garden with magnificent rhododendrons, azaleas, flowering trees and bulbs. Grounds include one mile beech avenue to sea, famous 'apple walk', Romanesque ruin of St Baldred's Church, views across parkland to Tyne estuary and Lammermuir Hills. Teas. Dogs on leish please. Tyninghame 1 mile.
Admission £3.00 OAPs £2.00 Children free
SUNDAYS 14 MAY & 25 JUNE 1 - 5pm
40% to Marie Curié Cancer Care - May Opening & to RNLI - June Opening
60% net to SGS Charities.

---

12. WINTON HOUSE, Pencaitland

(Sir Francis Ogilvy Winton Trust)
The Gardens have been substantially improved and extended in recent years extending down to Sir Davids Loch and up into the walled garden. In Spring there is a glorious covering of Daffodils and other colours making way for the cherry and apple blossoms. The café at Winton is well known for its excellent home baking and afternoon teas.
Entrance off B6355 Tranent/Pencaitland Road.
Admission: House tour & grounds: £5.00, OAPs £4.00, children under 10 free
Grounds & café only: £2.50,
SUNDAY 2 APRIL 12.30 - 4.30pm
The Princess Royal Trust for Carers 60% net to SGS Charities

---

13. SGS 10th ANNIVERSARY PLANT SALE - Joint opening East Lothian & Midlothian
held undercover at **OXENFOORD FARM,** Near Pathhead ♿
Excellent selection of garden and house plants donated from private gardens. Specialist plant stall, run by the NCCPG. Refreshments, home baking, fresh produce. Signed of A68 4 miles south of Dalkeith. Contact telephone number: Mrs Parker 01620 824788 or Mrs Baron 0131 663 1895.
SATURDAY 14 OCTOBER 9am- 2.30pm
40% to Cancer Research UK   60% net to SGS Charities

EDINBURGH & WEST LOTHIAN

Joint District Organisers: **Mrs Victoria Reid Thomas,** Riccarton Mains Farmhouse,
Currie EH14 4AR

Mrs Charles Welwood, Kirknewton House, Kirknewton,
West Lothian EH27 8DA

Hon. Treasurer: **Mrs Charles Welwood**

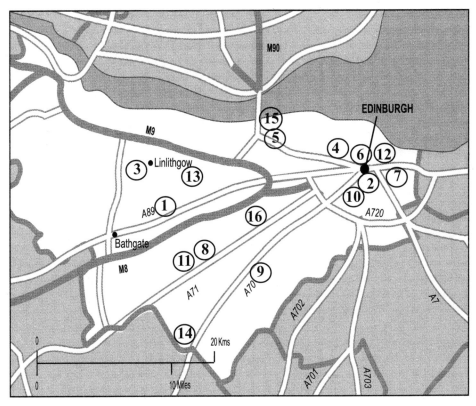

69

DATES OF OPENING

61 Fountainhall Road, Edinburgh .... By appointment
Annet House Garden. .... Easter - October Mon - Sat   10am - 5pm
.... Sundays   1 - 4pm
Kirknewton House, Kirknewton .... By appointment Monday - Friday
Newliston, Kirkliston .... Wed - Sun inc. 3 May - 4 June   2 - 6pm

Dalmeny Park, South Queensferry (Snowdrops) .... Sunday 19 February	2 - 5pm
61 Fountainhall Road, Edinburgh .... Sunday 2 April	2 - 5pm
Belgrave Crescent Gardens, Edinburgh .... Sunday 7 May	2 - 5pm
Dean Gardens, Edinburgh.. Sunday 7 May	2 - 5pm
61 Fountainhall Road, Edinburgh .... Sunday 21 May	2 - 5pm
Moray Place & Bank Gardens, Edinburgh .... Sunday 21 May	2 - 5pm
Suntrap Horticultural Centre, Edinburgh .... Sunday 28 May	10.30am - 5pm
Sawmill, Harburn.. Saturday 10 June	11am - 5pm
61 Fountainhall Road, Edinburgh .... Wednesday 21 June	6 - 9pm
Merchiston Cottage, 16 Colinton Road, Edinburgh .... Sunday 25 June	2 - 5pm
Mo Runlion, (My Secret Garden)............................. Sunday 25 June	1 - 6pm
South Queensferry Gardens. .... Sunday 2 July	2 - 5pm
Malleny Garden, Balerno .... Saturday 8 July	10 - 4pm
2 Houstoun Gardens, Uphall .... Sat & Sun 22 & 23 July`	2 - 4.30pm
Annet House, Linlithgow .... Sunday 30 July	10am - 5pm
Dr Neil's Garden, Duddingston .... Sat & Sun 5 & 6 August	2 - 5pm
61 Fountainhall Road, Edinburgh .... Sunday 3 September	2 - 5pm
61 Fountainhall Road, Edinburgh .... Sunday 8 October	2 - 5pm

✪ 1. **2 Houstoun Gardens, Uphall**
(John & Isabel Macdonald)
Small housing estate garden with scalloped front lawn, surrounded on three sides by annual &
bedding plants with shrubs & perennials on the fourth. The side and rear garden contain
perennials, fruit trees and bushes, a vegetable garden, oributal garden, rockery, patio, two pools
and a streeam. There is also a greenhouse and outdoor chess. The garden has over sixty
containers, baskets & pouches. Teas. Plant Stall. Route: from A89 turn onto B8046 (Uphall,
Broxburn) Turn right into Stankards Road, second left is Houstoun Gardens. Train to Uphall ½
mile walk down B8046. First Bus 16 to end of Stankards Road.
Admission £3.00   Children free
SATURDAY & SUNDAY 22 & 23 JULY 2 - 4.30pm
40% to Chest, Heart & Stroke Scotland 60% net to SGS Charities

2. 61 FOUNTAINHALL ROAD, Edinburgh

(Dr J A & Mrs A Hammondl)

Large walled town garden in which trees and shrubs form an architectural backdrop to a wide variety of flowering plants. The growing collection of hellebores and trilliums and the variety of late blooming flowers provide interest from early March to late October. As seen on the 'Beechgrove Garden' and the Chelsea Flower Show programme. 2 fish ponds have attracted a lively population of frogs. Plant Stall. Teas.

Admission £3.00 Children free

SUNDAYS 2 APRIL, 21 MAY, 3 SEPTEMBER & 8 OCTOBER 2 - 5pm
WEDNESDAY 21 JUNE 6 - 9pm (mid summer) Wine & nibbles.
ALSO by appointment. Tel: (0131) 667 6146
40% to Froglife   60% net to SGS Charities

---

3. ANNET HOUSE GARDEN, 143 High Street, Linlithgow

(The Linlithgow Story)

Restored terraced garden, situated to the rear and an integral part of Linlithgow's Museum has a wide range of flowers, fruit, vegetables and herbs, which were grown in the past to meet the culinary, medicinal and household needs of those who stayed in the house. Also see the unique life-size statue of Mary, Queen of Scots. Route: By road, turn off the M9 Stirling/Edinburgh, from the north - exit 4 from the south - exit 3. From the M8 - junction 4. Follow signs to Linlithgow. Bus & train services operate from Edinburgh & Glasgow. Situated in the High Street, close to the Palace, west of the Cross.

Admission £2.50 (includes entry to museum and refreshments)

SPECIAL SGS OPEN DAY SUNDAY 30 JULY 10am - 5pm
Also open Easter - October inclusive. Mon - Sat 10am -5pm Sun 1 - 4pm (Admission £1.50)
All takings to SGS Charities

---

4. BELGRAVE CRESCENT GARDENS, Edinburgh ♿ (partial)

(Belgrave Crescent Residents)

Privately owned city centre gardens of 7½ acres. Formal upper area with wooded slopes to Water of Leith and Dean Village. Teas. Plant Stall. Route: entrance from Belgrave Crescent East Gate bus no. 41 37 19

Admission £2.00 Children under 12 free

SUNDAY 7 MAY 2 - 5pm
40% to Alzheimer Scotland Edinburgh Branch 60% net to SGS Charities

---

5. DALMENY PARK, South Queensferry

(The Earl & Countess of Rosebery)

Acres of snowdrops on Mons Hill. Cars free. Teas will be available in the Courtyard Tearoom, Dalmeny House. Route: South Queensferry, off A90 road to B924. Pedestrians and cars enter by Leuchold Gate and exit by Chapel Gate. Please wear sensible footwear with good grip as paths can be slippy.

Admission £3.00 Children under 14 free

SUNDAY 19 FEBRUARY 2 - 5pm
40% to St Columba's Hospice 60% net to SGS Charities

---

6. DEAN GARDENS, Edinburgh
(Dean Gardens Committee of Management)
Privately owned town gardens on north bank of the Water of Leith. 13½ acres of spring bulbs, daffodils and shrubs. The Victorian pavilion has been reinstated and there is new seating throughout the garden. Entrance at Ann Street or Eton Terrace. New members welcome to Dean Gardens.
Admission £2.00 Children free
SUNDAY 7 MAY 2 - 5pm
40% to the Gardens Fund of the National Trust for Scotland   60% net to SGS Charities

---

7. DR NEIL'S GARDEN, Duddingston Village
(Dr Neil's Garden Trust)
Landscaped garden on the lower slopes of Arthur's Seat using conifers, heathers and alpines. Teas in Kirk Hall. Plant stalls. Car Park on Duddingston Road West. Dogs on leads please.
Admission £2.00 Children free.
SATURDAY & SUNDAY 5 & 6 AUGUST 2 - 5pm
40% to Dr Neil's Garden Trust   60% net to SGS Charities

---

8. KIRKNEWTON HOUSE, Kirknewton &
(Mr & Mrs Charles Welwood)
Old landscaped gardens, surrounded by mature trees. Shrubs, rhododendrons spring and herbaceous borders. Route: Either A71 or A70 on to B7031.
By Appointment Monday - Friday
Tel: 01506 881235 Email: cwelwood@kirknewtonestate.co.uk

✦ 9. MALLENY GARDEN, Balerno &   (no accessible toilet)
(National Trust for Scotland)
3 acre walled garden with 17th century clipped yew trees, lawns & borders. Wide & varied selection of herbaceous plants & shrubs. Shrub roses including NCCPG 19th century rose collection, ornamental vegetable & herb garden. Greenhouse display. Plant stall. Tea & Biscuits. Route in Balerno, off A70 Lanark Road. LRT No. 44   First Bus No. 44.
Admission £3.00 Children £2.00
SATURDAY 8 JULY 10am - 4pm
40% to NTS Gardens Fund 60% net to SGS Charities

---

10. MERCHISTON COTTAGE, 16 Colinton Road &   (most parts)
(Mr & Mrs H Mendelssohn)
This urban walled organic garden attempts to maximise space in a light hearted style. The eco friendly tapestry of wildlife habitats encourages small birds, insects, frogs and visiting ducks. Honey bees - sometimes visible in an observation hive. Teas and Plant Stall. Near 'Holy Corner' and Napier University, opposit George Watson's College. Buses: nos. 11 & 16.
Admission £3.00 Children free.
SUNDAY 25 JUNE 2 - 5pm
40% to Edinburgh Hebrew Community Centre 60% net to SGS Charities

⊛ **11. MO RUNLIOS, Kirknewton** (in part with assistance)
(Andrew & Heather Coutts)
Begun from a "blank canvas" plot of 1.2 acres in May 1999. This is now a 'working' country
garden comprising various themed areas (secrets) with great emphasis on nature, including a
large pond and a small wild flower meadow & stream, all surrounded by wildlife hedging. Teas.
Plant stall. Route: 1.5 miles south-west of Kirknewton on Leydon Road on the west side of
Kirknewton and the A70.
Admission £3.00 Children under 12 free.
SUNDAY 25 JUNE 1 - 6pm
40% to NTS Gardens Fund 60% net to SGS Charities

---

12. MORAY PLACE & BANK GARDENS, Edinburgh
Moray Place
Private garden of 3½ acres in Georgian New Town, recently benefitted from five-year programme
of replanting; shrubs, trees, and beds offering atmosphere of tranquillity in the city centre.
Entrance: north gate in Moray Place.
Bank Gardens
Nearly six acres of secluded wild gardens with lawns, trees and shrubs with banks of bulbs down
to the Water of Leith; stunning vistas across Firth of Forth. Entrance: gate at top of Doune
Terrace. Teas.
Admission £2.50 Children free
SUNDAY 21 MAY 2 - 5pm
40% to Marie Curie Cancer Care 60% net to SGS Charities

---

13. NEWLISTON, Kirkliston
(Mr & Mrs R C Maclachlan)
18th century designed landscape. Rhododendrons and azaleas. The house, which was designed
by Robert Adam, is open. Teas. On Sundays tea is in the Edinburgh School of food and wine
which operates in the William Adam Coach House. Also on Sundays there is a ride-on steam
model railway from 2 - 5 pm. Four miles from Forth Road Bridge, entrance off B800.
Admission to House & Garden £2.00 Children & OAPs £1.00
WEDNESDAYS - SUNDAYS inclusive each week
FROM 3 MAY - 4 JUNE 2 - 6pm
40% to Children's Hospice Association Scotland 60% net to SGS Charities

---

14. SAWMILL, Harburn
(Andrew Leslie)
Valley garden built around the ruins of an old water mill. Mixed planting, including herbaceous
and bog gardens, with azaleas and asiatic primulas. The garden is open in conjunction with the
Harburn Festival (Crafts, Art Exhibition, Dog Show, bouncy castle, etc.) Teas in Community
Hall. Dogs on a lead please. Plant stall. Route: A70 Edinburgh/Lanark road, or A71 to West
Calder, then B7008.
Admission £2.00 Children under 15 Free
SATURDAY 10 JUNE 11am - 5pm
40% to Harburn Village Hall 60% net to SGS Charitie

---

15. SOUTH QUEENSFERRY GARDENS
A group of gardens of varied size and design, with many surprises in the historic town of South Queensferry. Tickets and maps available *on the day* from **St. Mary's House, Kirkliston Road, South Queensferry** and **The Forts, Hawes Brae, South Queensferry.** Teas. Plant Stall.
Route: off A90, north of Edinburgh.
Admission £3.00
SUNDAY 2 JULY 2 - 5pm
40% to Care in the Community   60% net to SGS Charities

16. SUNTRAP EDINBURGH HORTICULTURAL & GARDENING CENTRE,
Gogarbank, Edinburgh ♿
(Oatridge Agricultural College, organised by Friends of Suntrap Edinburgh (NTS Members Centre)
A horticultural out-centre of Oatridge College. Compact garden of 1.7 hectares (3 acres), range of areas including rock and water features, sunken garden, raised beds, vegetable zone, woodland plantings & greenhouses. New home of the Scottish Bonsai Collection. Facilities for professional and amateur instruction, meeting and classroom facilities, horticultural advice and visitor interest. Signposted 0.5m west of Gogar roundabout, off A8 and 0.25m west of Calder Junction (City bypass) off A71. Bus route: Mactours No. 67. Open daily throughout the year until dusk. Plant sales Monday - Friday 9am -4.30pm. Friends of Suntrap Edinburgh programme of events - *www.ntscentres.org.uk/suntrap*. Advice/booking Tel: 0131 339 7283.
Family day out with plant sales, horticultural advice surgery, homebake teas, stalls and entertainment. Parking for disabled drivers inside main gate other parking opposite.
Admission £2.00 Children & OAPs £1.00
SUNDAY 28 MAY 10.30am - 5pm
20% to Perennial (GRBS) 20% to Friends of Suntrap   60% net to SGS Charities

ETTRICK & LAUDERDALE

District Organiser:	**Mrs D Muir**, Torquhan House, Stow TD1 2RX
Area Organiser:	**Mrs M Kostoris,** Wester Housebyres, Melrose TD6 9BW
Hon Treasurer:	**Mr Miller,** 18 Craigpark Gardens, Galashiels TD1 3HZ

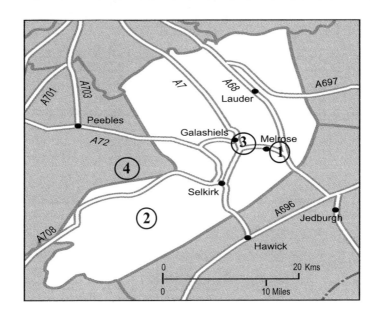

DATES OF OPENING

Bemersyde, Melrose	Sunday 23 April	2 - 5pm
Gattonside Village Gardens.	Sunday 25 June	2 - 5pm
Crosslee Old Farmhouse, Ettrick Valley and		
Netherphawhope.	Sunday 2 July	2 - 5pm
Old Tollhouse, Mountbenger, Yarrow	Sunday 13 August	2 - 5pm

1. BEMERSYDE, Melrose &

(The Earl Haig)
16th century peel tower reconstructed in the 17th century with added mansion house. Garden laid out by Field Marshal Earl Haig. Views of Eildon Hills. Woodland garden and river walks. Admission to garden only. Route: B6356. St Boswells via Clintmains or Melrose via Leaderfoot Bridge.
Admission £3.00   Children under 10 free
SUNDAY 23 APRIL 2 - 5pm
40% to Lady Haig's Poppy Factory   60% net to SGS Charities

---

2. CROSSLEE OLD FARMHOUSE, Ettrick Valley   &

(Dr & Mrs James Lockie)
Smallish organic walled garden at 900ft. Soft fruit, flowers, vegetables and herbs in raised beds. Children's play area. Treasure hunt with prizes. Aboretum. Wood with two streams. Erosion control. Picnic area. Dogs on leads please. Cream teas on south facing terrace. Plant stall. Route: from Edinburgh turn off at Innerleithen (B709). Remaining on B709 cross over at Gordon Arms Inn then turn left at next fork, over bridge, follow signs. From Selkirk turn left on to B7009 for 14 miles (pass through Ettrick Bridge at 7 mile mark) Follow signs for car park. A lovely drive 10 miles further up this beautiful and unknown valley to....

⊕ **NETHERPHAWHOPE** ♿

(Mr & Mrs Walter Barrie)

950ft exposed hill garden developed from scratch (grazed Hillside) in the last 20 years. Built on historic working hill farm. Vegetable tunnel, woodland & riverside walks, summerhouse & many different features..

Admission £3.50 Concessions £2.00

SUNDAY 2 JULY 2 - 5pm

40% to Amnesty International 60% net to SGS Charities

---

3. GATTONSIDE VILLAGE GARDENS ♿ (partly)

A selection of village gardens including;

Sunnyknowe, Bakers Road (Mr & Mrs Edward Dodd)

An old cottage garden which since 1996, has been gradually extended over a steep slope. Interesting selection of herbacious plants thrive on the well drained soil. Also roses and a small rockery.

Wildcroft (Mr & Mrs J Dalgleish)

Sunny south-facing garden with conifers, shrubs and various themed areas.

Avenel (Mr & Mrs I Purves)

South facing garden, mixed planting with a pond.

Govanbank (Mr & Mrs D Lyal)

Mature garden on south facing slope with pond and decking area.

Corners House, Hoebridge Road (Mr & Mrs AJ Brownlie)

Small seme-formal walled garden with the theme 'colour for 12 months of the year'.

Swallowbank (Mr and Mrs C Johnstone)

Mixed garden with themed areas.

Little Orchard (Eleanor Palmer)

South facing small garden of main street.

Willow Cottage (Moira Wright)

Traditional cottage garden opposite Little Orchard.

And others

Gattonside is two miles from Leaderfoot Bridge, on A68, north side of the River Tweed. Tickets from Village Hall (centre of village). Teas in village hall. Plant stall.

Admission £3.00 includes all gardens. Children free.

SUNDAY 25 JUNE 2-5pm

40% to Multiple Sclerosis 60% net to SGS Charities

⊕ **4. OLD TOLLHOUSE, Mountbenger, Yarrow**

(Victoria Harcastle & Iain Prain)

Small garden, approximately third of an acre, in elevated moor land situation. Bounded by a burn, it has been developed over the past 12 years using organic methods from rough moor land to create a cottage style garden. With mature and young trees, flower and vegetable garden, grasses, alpine garden, small pond, art works and seating areas. No dogs please, scares the ducks. Teas. Plant stall. Route: B709, 7 miles south of Innerleithen - 1 mile north Gordon Inn Hotel crossroads.

SUNDAY 13 AUGUST 2 - 6pm

40% to Amnesty International 60% net to SGS Charities

FIFE

District Organiser: **Mrs Catherine Erskine,** Cambo House, Kingsbarns KY16 8QD

Area Organisers: **Mrs Jeni Auchinleck,** 2 Castle Street, Crail KY10 3SQ
Mrs Evelyn Crombie, West Hall, Cupar KY15 4NA
Mrs Sue Eccles, Whinhill, Upper Largo KY8 5QS
Mrs Nora Gardner, Inverie, 36 West End, St Monans
Mrs Helen Gray, Arnot Tower, Leslie, KY6 3JQ
Mrs Gill Hart, Kirklands House, Saline KY12 9TS
Ms Louise Roger, Chesterhill, Boarhills, St Andrews KY16 8PP
Lady Spencer Nairn, Barham, Bow of Fife KY15 5RG
Mrs Marilyn Whitehead, Greenside, Leven KY8 5NU

Hon. Treasurer: **Mrs Fay Smith,** 37 Ninian Fields, Pittenweem, Anstruther KY10 2QU

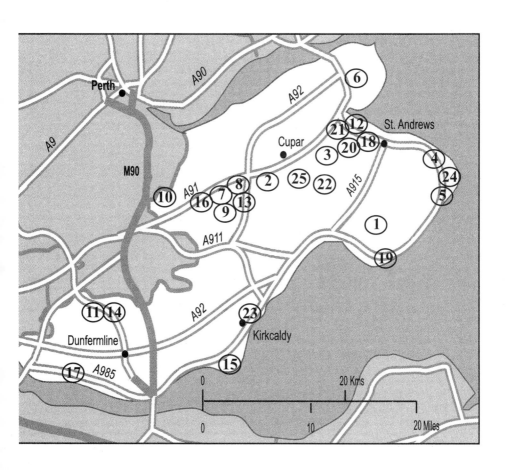

DATES OF OPENING

Cambo House, Kingsbarns	Open all year	10am - dusk
Strathtyrum, St Andrews	Weekdays 1st week of June	
	August & September	2 - 4.30pm
Wemyss Castle, East Wemyss	Open every Thursday mid	
	April to end August	12.30 - 6pm

Wemyss Castle, East Wemyss	Sunday 9 Apil	2 - 5pm
Spring Plant Fair, Cambo, Kingsbarns	Sunday 23 April	1 - 5pm
Barham, The Bow of Fife	Sunday 7 May	Noon - 5pm
Parleyhill Garden & Manse Garden, Culross.	Sunday 7 May	1- 5pm
Micklegarth, Aberdour	Sunday 14 May	2 - 5pm
Kirklands, Saline	Sunday 21 May	2 - 5pm
Falkland Small Gardens.	Sat & Sun 27 & 28 May	11.30 - 4.30pm
St Andrews Small Gardens.	Sunday 28 May	1 - 5pm
Gorno Grove House, by Strathmiglo	Sunday 28 May	2 - 5.30pm
St Monans Small Gardens.	Sunday 4 June	2 - 5pm
Balcarres, Colinsburgh	Saturday 10 June	2 - 5.30pm
Blebo Craigs Village, Cupar	Sunday 11 June	1 - 5pm
Micklegarth, Aberdour	Sunday 11 June	2 - 5pm
Freuchie Plant Sale .	Sunday 18 June	Noon - 4pm
Myres Castle, by Auchtermuchty	Thursday 22 June	5.30 - 8.30pm
Earlshall Castle, Leuchars	Sunday 25 June	2 - 5pm
Leckerston Cottage, Saline	Sunday 25 June	2 - 6pm
Lathrisk House,Old Lathrisk &		
North Lodge, Freuchie	Sunday 2 July	2 - 5.30pm
Micklegarth, Aberdour	Sunday 9 July	2 - 5pm
Teasses, Nr Ceres	Sunday 9 July	2 - 5pm
Wormistoune, Crail	Sunday 16 July	2 - 5.30pm
Earlshall Castle, Leuchars	Sunday 16 July	2 - 5pm
Crail Small Gardens.	Sat & Sun 22 & 23 July	1 - 5.30pm
Strathkinness Village Gardens.	Sat & Sun 29 & 30 July	2 - 5pm
Falkland Palace, Falkland	Sunday 20 August	1 - 5pm
Ladies Lake, St Andrews	Sunday 20 August	2 - 5pm
Cambo House, Kingsbarns	Sunday 17 September	2 - 5pm
Annual Plant Sale and Fair, Hill of Tarvit	Sunday 8 October	10.30 - 4.30pm

1. BALCARRES, Colinsburgh
(The Earl and Countess of Crawford and Balcarres)
19th Century formal and woodland garden; wide variety of plants. Teas. Plant stall. ½ mile north of Colinsburgh off A942.
Admission £3.50 Accompanied children free
SATURDAY 10 JUNE 2 - 5.30pm
20% to Maggie's Centre 20% to SWRI   60% net to SGS Charities

2. BARHAM, Bow of Fife   ♿

(Sir Robert & Lady Spencer Nairn)
A garden full of character and friends. A small woodland garden in the making with rhododendrons, shrubs spring bulbs and ferns. Plant stall. Hot soup and rolls. Route: A91, 4 miles west of Cupar. No dogs please.
Admission £3.50 Children under 12 free
SUNDAY 7 MAY 12 - 5pm
40% to Pain Association Scotland 60% net to SGS Charities

---

3. BLEBO CRAIGS VILLAGE GARDENS, Cupar   ♿ (partially)

(Blebo Craigs Village)
Blebo Craigs is a former quarry and farm village, with stunning views over the Fife countryside and lovely walks along country lanes. We will be opening three new gardens this year, along with several previous favourites, including the potter's garden with quarry lake and profusion of rhododendrons, a stunning organic garden, and a cottage garden with an abundance of colour and variety. Teas. Plant stall. Route: off the B939 between Cupar and St Andrews.
Admission £3.50 Children free
SUNDAY 11 JUNE 1 - 5pm
40% to Blebo Craigs Village Hall 60% net to SGS Charities

---

4. CAMBO HOUSE, Kingsbarns   ♿ (Partial)

(Peter & Catherine Erskine)
Romantic Victorian walled garden designed around the Cambo burn with willow, waterfall and charming wrought-iron bridges. Ornamental potager, breathtaking snowdrops (mail order in February) massed spring bulbs, lilac walk, naturalistic plantings, woodland garden, old roses, colchicum meadow and glowing autumn borders, All seasons plantsman's paradise. Woodland walks to the sea. Featured in 'Country Life' and 'The Garden'. Dogs on leads please. Route: A917.
Admission £3.50 Children free
SUNDAY 23 APRIL 1 - 5pm - Spring Plant and Craft Fair. Teas.
40% to Diabetes UK 60% net to SGS Charities
SUNDAY 17 SEPTEMBER 2 - 5pm - September Opening Teas, Plant stall.
All proceeds to SGS Charities
OPEN ALL YEAR ROUND 10am - dusk

---

5. CRAIL: SMALL GARDENS IN THE BURGH

(The Gardeners of Crail)
A number of small gardens in varied styles: cottage, historic, plantsman's, bedding. Plant stall. Approach Crail from either St Andrews or Anstruther, A917. Park in the Marketgate. Tickets and map available from Mrs Auchinleck, 2 Castle Street, Crail and Mr and Mrs Robertson - The Old House, 9 Marketgate. No dogs please.
Admission £3.50 Acccompanied Children free
SATURDAY & SUNDAY 22 & 23 JULY 1 - 5.30pm
20% to Crail British Legion Hall Fund 20% to Crail Preservation Society 60% net to SGS Charities

6. EARLSHALL CASTLE, Leuchars

(Paul & Josine Veenhuijzen)

Garden designed by Sir Robert Lorimer. Topiary lawn for which Earlshall is renowned, rose terrace, croquet lawn with herbaceous borders, shrub border, box garden and orchard. No dogs please. Teas and plant stall. Route: On Earlshall road ¾ of a mile east of Leuchars Village (off A919).

Admission £3.50 Children free

SUNDAY 25 JUNE 2 - 5pm

40% to The Liberating Scots Trust 60% net to SGS Charities

SUNDAY 16 JULY 2 - 5.pm

40% to The Princess Royal Trust for Carers 60% net to SGS Charities

---

7. FALKLAND - SMALL GARDENS OF THE ROYAL BURGH ☍ (some)

Enjoy walking around the Royal Burgh visiting interesting, very varies, small gardens and chat with the owners. Tickets from Maspie House, High Street, Falkland. Several tearooms in Burgh.

Admission £3.50

SATURDAY & SUNDAY 27 & 28 MAY 11.30am - 4.30pm

20% to Maggie's Centre 20% to Childhood Liver Disease Foundation 60% net to SGS Charities

---

8. FALKLAND PALACE GARDEN, Falkland ☍

(The National Trust for Scotland)

The Royal Palace of Falkland, set in the heart of a medieval village, was the country residence and hunting lodge of eight Stuart monarchs, including Mary, Queen of Scots. The palace gardens were restored by the late Keeper, Major Michael Crichton Stuart, to a design by Percy Cane. Tearooms nearby in village. Free car park in village. Route: A912.

Admission to Garden £5.00 Family ticket £12.50

For Palace admission prices and concessions please see the NTS advert at back of book

SUNDAY 20 AUGUST 1 - 5pm

40% to The Gardens Fund of the National Trust for Scotland 60% net to SGS Charities

---

9. FREUCHIE PLANT SALE 🚗 (with help)

(Major & Mrs A B Cran)

A wide selection of plants: Perennial and bedding will be on sale at Karbet in the centre of Freuchie on the B936. Refreshments.

Admission £1.00 Children free

SUNDAY 18 JUNE Noon - 4pm

40% to SSAFA Forces Help 60% net to SGS Charities

---

10. GORNO GROVE HOUSE, by Strathmiglo ☍ (if dry)

(Sandy & Dianne Matthew)

7 acre developing woodland garden, swathes of mixed native trees with grass paths and avenues. Good views to Lomond hills. A collection of young rhododendrons, azaleas and other shrubs. There is also a pond with water plants and a burn. Plant stall. Soup and rolls, Teas/Coffee and scones. Route: off A91, 1 mile east of Gateside. Dogs on leads please. Jazz Band 2 - 4pm

Admission £3.00 Children free

SUNDAY 28 MAY 2 - 5.30pm

40% to CHAS 60% net to SGS Charities

---

11. KIRKLANDS, Saline   ♿ (partial)

(Peter & Gill Hart)

Kirklands has been developed and restored over the last 28 years, although the house dates from 1832. Herbaceous borders, bog garden, woodland garden with fern collection and walled garden (gradually being restored). New recently planted woodland area. Saline Burn divides the garden from the ancient woodland and woodland walk. Teas and Plant Stall. Route: Junction 4 M90 then B914. Parking in the centre of the village. Dogs on a lead please.

Admission £3.00 Accompanied children free

SUNDAY 21 MAY 2 - 5pm

40% to Saline Environmental Group   60% net to SGS Charities

---

12. LADIES LAKE, The Scores, St Andrews   ♿ (with help - some steps)

(Mr and Mrs Gordon T Senior)

The garden is small, no more than half an acre. It occupies a saucer-shaped curve on the cliff adjacent to St Andrews Castle. In essence, the garden consists of two terraces, one of which is cantilevered over the sea. About 6,000 bedding plants are crammed into half a dozen beds. Teas provided by the ladies of Hope Park Church. Plant stall. Music. Route: from North Street, turn left into North Castle Street, left in front of castle and house is 150 yards on right.

Admission £3.00 Accompanied children free

SUNDAY 20 AUGUST 2 - 5pm

40% to Hope Park Church, St Andrews   60% net to SGS Charities

---

13. LATHRISK HOUSE, OLD LATHRISK & NORTH LODGE, Freuchie ♿ (access with help)

(Mrs David Skinner, Mr & Mrs David Wood, Mr & Mrs Mike Aitken)

First opening since 2002, which has allowed considerable developments in these very different and beautiful gardens, surrounding houses dating from the 17th century, in a peaceful rural setting, favoured by monks in the 12th century. Really good plant stall. Teas in marquees. Traditional Jazz. Easy parking. No dogs please.

Admission £4.00 Children free.

SUNDAY 2 JULY 2 - 5.30pm

40% to Falkland & Freuchie Parish Church   60% net to SGS Charities

---

❃ 14. LECKERSTON COTTAGE, Saline   ♿ (with help to access garden)

(David & Margaret Farmer)

New garden of 10 growing seasons embracing an oriental style. Contains trees, shrubs, perennial plants, large wildlife pond & ornamental ponds. Adjoining wild garden. Teas. Plant stall. No dogs. Route: ½ mile from Saline Post Office on Bridge Street.

Admission £2.50 Children free.

SUNDAY 25 JUNE 2 - 6pm

40% to Home Start, Dunfermline   60% net to SGS Charities

---

15. MICKLEGARTH, Aberdour

(Gordon & Kathleen Maxwell)

Informal village garden of 30 plus years standing; island beds of mixed herbacious and shrubs, with winding paths. Plant stall. No dogs.

Admission £2.50

SUNDAY'S 14 MAY, 11 JUNE & 9 JULY 2 - 5pm

May & July 40% to Maggie's Centre, Fife   June 40% to Home Start, Dunfermline
60% net to SGS Charities

---

16. MYRES CASTLE, Auchtermuchty   ♿ *(gravel drive)*
(Mr & Mrs Jonathan White)
Formal walled gardens laid out in the style of the Vatican gardens in Rome to reflect the Fairlie family's papal connections.   Plant stall.   No dogs.   Route: On the B936, off the A91
Admission £7.50   includes glass of wine & canapes
THURSDAY 22 JUNE 5.30 - 8.30pm
40% to Falkland Heritage Trust   60% net to SGS Charities

---

17. PARLEYIIILL GARDEN & MANSE GARDEN Culross   ♿
(Mr & Mrs R J McDonald   &   Revd & Mrs T Moffat)
Overlooking the Forth and the historic village of Culross both these gardens nestle in the shade of Culross Abbey and the adjacent Abbey ruins. Parleyhill Garden has evolved in two parts, the earlier in the mid - 60s, the latter in the late 80's. The garden of the Abbey Manse is situated in the old Abbey cloister garden.   Both are delightful hidden gardens bordered by stone walls with interesting displays of old fashioned herbaceous perennials and a good variety of seasonal plants, bulbs and shrubs.   Good plant stall selling plants from the gardens.   Teas.   Guide dogs only. Disabled access to Parleyhill Garden and Manse tearoom.   Parking at the Abbey and in the village.
Admission £3.50   Accompanied children free
SUNDAY 7 MAY 1 - 5pm
40% to Culross and Torryburn Church   60% net to SGS Charities

---

18. ST. ANDREWS SMALL GARDENS
An interesting selection of 'hidden gardens' in the Hepburn Gardens and Lade Braes area of St Andrews.   Tickets from Littleridge, Hepburn Gardens and 32 Lade Braes.   Parking along Hepburn Gardens and in Argyll Street car park.   Teas at Littleridge.   Plant Stall.
Admission £3.50 Accompanied children free.
SUNDAY 28 MAY 1 - 5pm
40% to Prostate Cancer Charity   60% net to SGS Charities

---

19. ST. MONANS SMALL GARDENS
A number of gardens in this seaside village, with intriguing views of the sea.   Familiar gardens and additional new gardens this year.   Hidden, enclosed ones and others open to the sea.   Prize winning vegetable gardens and a new water garden.   Tickets and map available from Inverie, 36 West End, situated on the hill above the Auld Kirk.   Parking at church and east of the harbour. Teas in Church hall, Station Road.   Good plant stall in 'Inverie'.
Admission Adults £3.00   Accompanied children free.
SUNDAY 4 JUNE 2 - 5pm
40% to St Monans Auld Kirk   60% net to SGS Charities

---

20. STRATHKINNESS VILLAGE GARDENS
A number of varied and interesting gardens in the village which also enjoys panoramic views over the Eden Estuary and St Andrews.   Tickets and maps from the Village Hall on Main Street Street parking.   Teas and plant stall in hall.   Route: approx 3 miles from St Andrews on the B939 and signposted on the A91 on leaving Guardbridge for St Andrews.
Admission £3.50 Accompanied children free
SATURDAY & SUNDAY 29 & 30 JULY 2 -5pm
40% Strathkinness Church   60% net to SGS Charities

21. STRATHTYRUM, St Andrews   ♿

(Mr and Mrs A Cheape)

Gardens surrounding house, including small rose garden and newly restored four acre walled garden. Route: Large iron gates with grey urns on right of A91 - ½ mile before St Andrews on Guardbridge side.

Admission £3.00 (House open - Admission £5.00 Child £2.50)

Garden open weekdays, first week of JUNE, AUGUST & SEPTEMBER 2-4.30pm

40% Maggie's Centre   60% net to SGS Charities

---

22. TEASSES HOUSE, nr Ceres

(Sir Fraser and Lady Morrison)

Victorian building of 1879, completely restored in 1996. House gardens and oval walled kitchen garden (disused for many years) under restoration. Newly laid out terrace garden: meadow garden with mown grass lawn, avenue walk and amphitheatre. Woodland and mown grass walks. Woodlands being reinstated to provide sustainable flora and fauna, containing some unusual ornamental plants and small individual gardens for each family member. Rose garden and children's garden. Teas. Plant stall. No dogs please. Route: 2 miles south of Ceres on the Lundin Links / Largo Road.

Admission £3.50 Children free

SUNDAY 9 JULY 2 - 5pm

40% to Barnardos   60% net to SGS Charities

---

23. WEMYSS CASTLE, East Wemyss

(Michael and Charlotte Wemyss)

Woodland garden remarkable for its wonderful display of Erythronium revolutum and spring bulbs. Six acre walled garden in the process of complete restoration, begun in 1994 and still ongoing. There are many herbaceous borders with a large collection of roses and clematis. Teas. Plant stall. Dogs welcome on a lead. Route A955 1 mile south of East Wemyss.

Admission £4.00 Children Free

SUNDAY 9 APRIL 2 - 5pm

40% to The Wemyss School of Needlework.   60% net to SGS Charities

Also open every Thursday 12.30 - 6pm mid April - end August.

---

24. WORMISTOUNE, Crail

(James & Gemma McCallum of Wormistoune)

17th century formal walled and woodland garden. New Pleasance Garden and mosaic celtic cross. Splendid herbaceous border. Largest listed Grisselinia in Scotland. Teas and plant stall. Route: On A917 Crail - St Andrews. No dogs please.

Admission £3.50 Children free

SUNDAY 16 JULY 2 - 5.30pm

40% to Barnardos   60% net to SGS Charities

---

25. ANNUAL SGS PLANT SALE AND FAIR at Hill of Tarvit, by Cupar

(The National Trust for Scotland)

Interesting selection of plants and clumps of herbaceous plants at bargain prices. Food and Craft Fair. Gardener's Question Time. Refreshments. Route: A916.

SUNDAY 8 OCTOBER 10.30 - 4.30pm

40% to East Fife Members Centre of The National Trust for Scotland 60% net to SGS Chariti

---

GLASGOW & DISTRICT

District Organiser: **Mrs V A Field,** Killorn, 8 Baldernock Road, Milngavie G62 8DR

Area Organisers: **Mrs A Barlow,** 5 Auchencruive, Milngavie G62 6EE
        Mrs M Collins, Acre Valley House, Torrance G64 4DJ
        Mrs C M T Donaldson, 2 Edgehill Road, Bearsden G61 3AD
        Mr A Heasman, 76 Sandhead Terrace, Blantyre G72 0JH
        Mrs A Murray, 44 Gordon Road, Netherlee G44 5TW
        Mr Alan Simpson, 48 Thomson Drive, Bearsden G61 3NZ
        Mrs A C Wardlaw, 92 Drymen Road, Bearsden G61 2SY

Hon. Treasurer: **Mr J Murray,** 44 Gordon Road, Netherlee G44 5TW

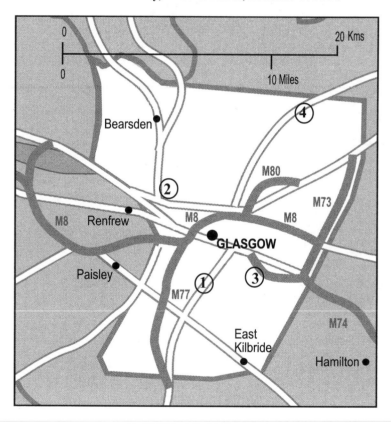

DATES OF OPENING

Invermay, Cambuslang .... April - September by appointment

Glasgow Botanic Gardens. .... Saturday 10 June   11am - 4pm
Kilsyth Gardens . ... Sunday 11 June   2 - 5pm
46 Corrour Road, Newlands .... Sunday 18 June   2 - 5pm

1. 46 CORROUR ROAD, Newlands
(Robert & Shona Elliot)
A beautiful town garden skillfully developed over many years to provide all year interest with
low maintenance. The emphasis is on shrubs and perennials with varied leaf shape colour and
texture carefully grouped together with dramatic effect. Many unusual species, and numerous
changes since our last opening. Light refreshments. Some surplus plants may be available for
sale. Guide dogs only please. Access from Newlands Road off the A77 Kilmarnock Road near
St. Margaret's Church. Featured in best back gardens in Britain
Admission: £4.00 Children over 12 £1.00
SUNDAY 18 June 2 - 5pm
40% Muscular Dystrophy Campaign   60% net to SGS Charities

---

2. GLASGOW BOTANIC GARDENS
(Glasgow City Council)
Glasgow District's Annual Plant Sale will again be held in the spring. A large selection of indoor
and outdoor plants and shrubs will be for sale. There will also be an opportunity to view the
national Collection of Begonias and the extensive propogation areas. Scotland's largest collection
of filmy ferns set in a fairy like grotto will also be open to view and this is particularly appealing
to children. Refreshments available. Route: Leave M8 at Junction 17, follow signs for
Dumbarton. The Botanic Garden is at the junction of Great Western Road A82 and Queen
Margaret Drive.
Any donation of plants beforehand would be welcome: Please contact 0141 942 1295
Admission: Free
SATURDAY 10 JUNE 11am - 4pm
25% to Friends of the Botanics   75% net to SGS Charities

---

3. INVERMAY, 48 Wellshot Drive, Cambuslang
(Mrs M Robertson)
A plant lovers' garden. Wide variety of unusual bulbs, rock plants, herbaceous plants, shrubs
(many named) in a very sheltered, suburban garden. Greenhouse with fuchsias. Something in
flower all through the year - a special town garden. Teas. Plant Stall. A730 (East Kilbride) or
A749/A724 (Hamilton) from Glasgow. Convenient to M74/M73. Wellshot Drive starts at back
of Cambuslang Station.
Admission £2.50 Children over 12 £1.00
APRIL - SEPTEMBER Groups by appointment, please telephone first: 0141 641 1632
40% to Children First   60% net to SGS Charities

---

4. KILSYTH GARDENS
Aeolia (Mr & Mrs G Murdoch)   **Blackmill** (Mr John Patrick)
Aeolia has a garden of a third of an acre developed since 1960 by the present owners and
contains many mature specimen trees and shrubs, a large variety of rhododendrons, primulas,
hardy geraniums and herbaceous plants.
Blackmill is on the opposite side of the road from Aeolia and has an acre of ground developed on
the site of an old mill. Half of the garden has mature and recent plantings, an ornamental mill
and pond with the other half consisting of a natural wood and a glen with a cascading waterfall.
Plant stall. Toilets. No dogs please. Route: Take A803 to Kilsyth, turn northwards into
Parkburn Road and then follow signs from top of hill.
Admission to both gardens including home made tea £5.00 Children free
SUNDAY 11 JUNE 2-5pm
40% to Strathcarron Hospice 60% net to SGS Charities

ISLE OF ARRAN

District Organiser: **Mrs S C Gibbs,** Dougarie, Isle of Arran KA27 8EB

Hon. Treasurer: **Mr D Robertson,** Bank of Scotland, Brodick KA27 8AL

DATES OF OPENING

Dougarie. .... Sunday 2 July	2 - 5pm
Brodick Castle & Country Park .... Saturday 15 July	10am - 5pm
Brodick Castle & Country Park .... Saturday 12 August	10am - 5pm

1. BRODICK CASTLE & COUNTRY PARK   ♿ (some)
(The National Trust for Scotland)
Exotic plants and shrubs. Walled garden. Woodland garden. Car park free. Morning coffee,
lunch and tea available in Castle. NTS shop. Brodick 2 miles. Service buses from Brodick Pier
to Castle. Regular sailings from Ardrossan and from Claonaig (Argyll). Information from
Caledonian MacBrayne, Gourock.
Tel: 01475 650100.
SATURDAYS 15 JULY & 12 AUGUST 10am - 5pm
40% to The Gardens Fund of the National Trust for Scotland   60% net to SGS Charities

---

2. DOUGARIE
(Mr & Mrs S C Gibbs)
Terraced garden in castellated folly. Shrubs, herbaceous borders, traditional kitchen garden.
Tea. Produce stall. Blackwaterfoot 5 miles. Regular ferry sailing from Ardrossan and from
Claonaig (Argyll). Information from Caledonian MacBrayne, Gourock. Tel: 01475 650100.
Admission £2.00 Children 50p
SUNDAY 2 JULY 2 - 5pm
40% to an Island Charity   60% net to SGS Charities

KINCARDINE & DEESIDE

District Organiser:	**Mrs E L Hartwell,** Burnigill, Burnside, Fettercairn AB30 1XY
Area Organisers:	**The Hon Mrs J K O Arbuthnott,** Kilternan, Arbuthnott, Laurencekirk AB30 1NA
	Mrs D White, Lys-na-greyne House, Aboyne AB34 5JD
Hon. Treasurer:	**Mrs N Linday,** Muirside of Thornton, Laurencekirk. AB30 1EE

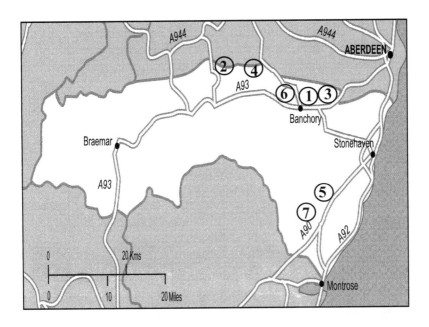

DATES OF OPENING

Inchmarlo House Garden, Banchory	Sunday 28 May	1.30 - 5pm
The Burn House, Glenesk	Sunday 4 June	2 - 5pm
Crathes Castle, Banchory	Sunday 25 June	2 - 5pm
Findrack, Torphins	Sunday 9 July	2 - 5pm
Drum Castle, Drumoak	Sunday 16 July	10 - 6pm
Douneside House, Tarland	Sunday 23 July	2 - 5pm
Glenbervie House, Drumlithie	Sunday 6 August	2 - 5pm

1. CRATHES CASTLE, Banchory &

(The National Trust for Scotland)
This historic castle and its gardens are situated near Banchory, in a delightful part of Royal Deeside. Crathes was formerly the home of Sir James & Lady Burnett, whose lifelong interests found expression in the gardens and in one of the best plant collections in Britain. No less than eight colourful gardens can be found within the walled garden. Exhibitions, shop and licensed restaurant. Sale of plants, garden walks, ranger walks, forest walks. Situated off A93, 3 miles east of Banchory, 15 miles west of Aberdeen.
Admission quoted includes castle, garden, estate and use of all facilities. A timed entry system to the castle applies to all visitors to avoid overcrowding in smaller rooms but there is no restriction on time spent inside. Castle tickets can be obtained on arrival.
Admission (Combined Ticket) £10.00 Child/Concs £7.00 Family £25.00 NTS/NT Members Free Gardens only £7.00 Car Park £2.00
SUNDAY 25 JUNE 1.30 - 5pm (Last entry to castle 4.45pm)
40% to The Gardens Fund of The National Trust for Scotland 60% net to SGS Charities

2. DOUNESIDE HOUSE, Tarland &

(The MacRobert Trust)
Ornamental and rose gardens around a large lawn with uninterrupted views to the Deeside Hills and Grampians; large, well-stocked vegetable garden, beech walks, water gardens and new glasshouses. Cars free. Tea in house. Plant stall. Local pipe band. Tarland 1½ miles. Route: B9119 towards Aberdeen.
Admission £2.50 Children & OAPs £1.00
SUNDAY 23 JULY 2 - 5pm
40% to Perennial (GRBS - Netherbyres Appeal) 60% net to SGS Charities

3. DRUM CASTLE, Drumoak, by Banchory &

(The National Trust for Scotland)
In the walled garden the Trust has established a collection of old-fashioned roses which is at its peak during July. The pleasant parkland contains the 100-acre Old Wood of Drum and offers fine views and walks. Garden walk 3pm. Route: 10 miles west of Aberdeen and 8 miles east of Banchory on A93.
Garden & Grounds only £3.00 Children £2.00
SUNDAY 16 JULY 10 - 6pm
40% to The Gardens Fund of The National Trust for Scotland 60% net to SGS Charities

4. FINDRACK, Torphins & (in parts)

(Mr and Mrs Andrew Salvesen)
Carefully redesigned over the last 12 years the gardens of Findrack are set in beautiful wooded countryside and are a haven of interesting plants and unusual design features. There is a walled garden with circular lawns and deep herbaceous borders, stream garden leading to a widlife pond, vegetable garden and woodland walk. Teas. Plant stall. Leave Torphins on A980 to Lumphanan after ½ mile turn off, signposted Tornaveen. Stone gateway 1mile up on left.
Admission £2.00 Children 50p
SUNDAY 9 JULY 2 - 5pm
40% to "The Breadmaker" Aberdeen 60% net to SGS Charities

5. GLENBERVIE HOUSE, Drumlithie, Stonehaven

(Mr & Mrs A Macphie)
Nucleus of present day house dates from the 15th century. Additions in 18th and 19th centuries. A traditional Scottish walled garden on a slope with roses, herbaceous and annual borders and fruit and vegetables. One wall is taken up with a fine Victorian conservatory with many varieties of pot plants and climbers on the walls, giving a dazzling display. There is also a woodland garden by a burn with primulas and ferns. Teas. Plant and baking stalls. Drumlithie 1 mile. Garden 1½ miles off A90. NOT SUITABLE FOR WHEELCHAIRS.
Admission £3.00 Children £1 Cars free
SUNDAY 6 AUGUST 2 - 5pm
40% to Aberdeen Renal Research Fund 60% net to SGS Charities

---

6. INCHMARLO HOUSE GARDEN, Banchory   ♿ (limited)

(Skene Enterprises (Aberdeen) Ltd)
An ever changing 5 acre woodland garden within Inchmarlo Continuing Care Retirement Community. Originally planted in the early Victorian era, featuring ancient Scots pines, Douglas firs, yews, beeches and a variety of other trees which form a dramatic background to an early summer riot of mature azaleas and rhododendrons producing a splendour of colour and scents. Tea, coffee, homebakes - £3. Route: From Aberdeen via North Deeside Road on A93 1mile west of Banchory, turn right at main gate to Inchmarlo House.
Admission £2.00 Children free
SUNDAY 28 MAY 1.30 - 5pm
40% to Alzheimer Scotland Action on Dementia   60% net to SGS Charities

---

7. THE BURN HOUSE & THE BURN GARDEN HOUSE, Glenesk   ♿

(Lt. Col and Mrs G A Middlemiss for The Burn Educational Trust)
The Burn House built in 1791 Grounds of 190 acres including 2½ mile river path by River North Esk and a beautiful walled garden. Tea, stalls and live music in Mansion House. Route: 1 mile north of Edzell. Front gate situated on North side of River North Esk bridge on B966.
Admission £2.50 Children under 12 free
SUNDAY 4 JUNE 2 - 5pm
40% to Cancer Research 60% net to SGS Charities

LOCHABER, BADENOCH & STRATHSPEY

Joint District Organisers: **Norrie & Anna Maclaren,** Ard-Daraich, Ardgour,
Nr Fort Wiliam PH33 7AB

Hon. Treasurer: **Anna Maclaren**

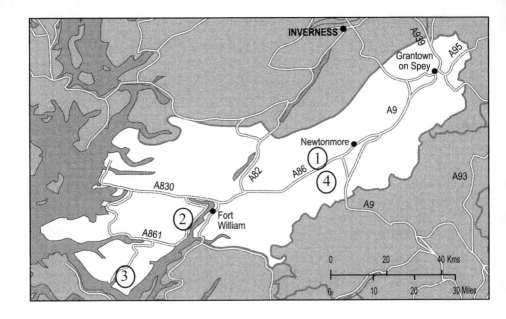

DATES OF OPENING

Ardtornish, Lochaline, Morvern .... Open 1 April - 31 October   10am - 6pm

Aberarder, Kinlochlaggan .... Sunday 28 May   2 - 5.30pm
Ardverikie, Kinlochlaggan .... Sunday 28 May   2 - 5.30pm
Ard-Daraich, Ardgour .... Sat & Sun 10 & 11 June   2 - 5.30pm

1. ABERARDER, Kinlochlaggan (Joint opening with Ardverikie)
(The Feilden Family)
Lovely garden and views over Loch Laggan. Home made teas. On A86 between Newtonmore and Spean Bridge at east end of Loch Laggan.
Combined admission with **ARDVERIKIE** £3.00. Children under 12 free
SUNDAY 28 MAY 2 - 5.30pm
20% to Marie Curie Cancer Care   20% to Laggan Church   60% net to SGS Charities

2. ARD-DARAICH, Ardgour, by Fort William ♿ (in places)
(Norrie & Anna Maclaren)
Seven acre hill garden, in a spectacular setting, with many fine and uncommon rhododendrons, an interesting selection of trees and shrubs and a large collection of camellias, acers and sorbus. Home made teas in house. Cake and plant stall. Route: West from Fort William, across the Corran Ferry, turn left and a mile on the right further west.
Admission £3.00 Children under 12 £1.00
SATURDAY/SUNDAY 10/11 JUNE 2 - 5.30pm
40% to Highland Hospice 60% net to SGS Charities

3. ARDTORNISH, by Lochaline, Morvern

(Mrs John Raven)
Garden of interesting mature conifers, rhododendrons, deciduous trees, shrubs and herbaceous
set amidst magnificent scenery. Route A884. Lochaline 3 miles
Entrance fee charged
OPEN 1 APRIL - 31 OCTOBER 10am - 6pm
Donation to Scotland's Gardens Scheme

---

4. ARDVERIKIE, Kinlochlaggan (Joint opening with Aberarder) &

(Mrs P Laing & Mrs E T Smyth Osbourne)
Lovely setting on Loch Laggan with magnificent trees. Walled garden with large collection of
acers, shrubs and herbaceous. Architecturally interesting house (Not open). Site of the filming of
the TV series "Monarch of the Glen". On A86 between Newtonmore and Spean Bridge.
Entrance at east end of Loch Laggan by gate lodge over bridge. Plant Stall. Home made teas at
Aberarder.
Combined admission with **ABERARDER** £3.00 Children 12 free
SUNDAY 28 MAY 2 - 5.30pm
20% to Marie Curie Cancer Care 20% to Laggan Church 60% net to SGS Charities

---

MIDLOTHIAN

District Organisers:	**Mrs Richard Barron,** Laureldene, Kevock Road, Lasswade EH18 1HT
Area Organisers:	**Mrs A M Gundlach,** Fermain, 4 Upper Broomieknowe, Lasswade EH18 1LP
	Mrs R Hill, 27 Biggar Road, Silverburn EH26 9LJ
	Mrs E Watson, Newlandburn House, Newlandrig, Gorebridge EH23 4NS
Hon. Treasurer:	**Mr A M Gundlach,** Fermain, 4 Upper Broomieknowe, Lasswade EH18 1LP

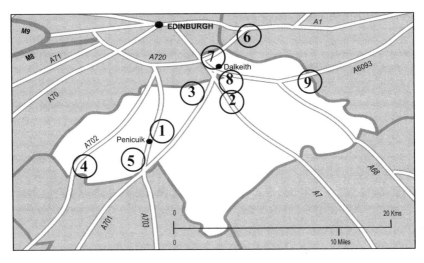

DATES OF OPENING

The Old Sun Inn, Newbattle .... Open by Appointment (most days)
.... 1 May - 30 July Tel: 0131 663 2648

Auchindinny House, Penicuik .... Sunday 4 June	2 - 5pm
The Old Parsonage & Brae House. .... Sunday 11 June	2 - 5.30pm
Lasswade: 16 Kevock Road .... Sat & Sun 17 & 18 June	2 - 5pm
Newhall, Carlops .... Sunday 18 June	11am - 4pm
Barondale House, Newbatle .... Sat & Sun 8 & 9 July	2 - 5pm
Newhall, Carlops .... Sunday 9 July	5.30 - 8.30pm
Pomathorn Gardens, Nr. Penicuik .... Sunday 6 August	2 - 5pm
SGS 10th Anniversary Plant Sale. .... Saturday 14 October	9am - 2.30pm
Rosecourt, Inveresk .... Sunday 3 December	11am - 3pm

1 AUCHINDINNY HOUSE, Penicuik   ♿ (partly)

(Mr & Mrs John McCulloch)

Formal avenue leading to a William Bruce house constructed between 1702 and 1707. One of the earliest non-fortified country houses in Scotland which has been continuously occupied by the same family for three hundred year. (House not open). Wild garden with rhododendrons, azaleas and woodland walk. Refreshments available. Route: on the B7026 at the southern end of Auchendinny Village.

Admission £2.50 Children under 12 free.

SUNDAY 4 JUNE 2.00 - 5.00pm

40% to Glencorse Parish Church 60% net to SGS Charities

---

2. BARONDALE HOUSE, Newbattle (Organic Garden)   ♿

(Alec & Diana Milne)

Half acre organic cottage garden attractively situated by River South Esk, providing year round fruit and vegetables. Old roses and lilies lead to marigolds which help the potatoes and nasturtiums climb the pea nets; slug-eating frogs hide under the waterlilies in the small pond and tagetes keeps whitefly at bay in the greenhouse. Plant stall. Route: 8 miles south of Edinburgh on B703 Newbattle/Eskbank Road.

Admission £2.50 Children free.

SATURDAY & SUNDAY 8 & 9 July 2 - 5pm

40% to Henry Doubleday Research Association   60% net to SGS Charities

---

3. LASSWADE: 16 Kevock Road

(David and Stella Rankin)

A hillside garden overlooking the North Esk Valley and the ruins of Mavisbank House, with many mature trees, rhododendrons, azaleas and unusual shrubs. These are underplanted with a wide range of woodland plants and there are ponds with primula, iris and other damp loving plants. Higher up the south facing slope there are terraces with rockeries and troughs. The garden has featured in several television programmes and magazine articles. A large plant stall featuring many specialist plants is a feature of this opening. Teas in Drummond Grange Nursing Home should be taken by 4pm (No. 3 Kevock Road) where cars may be parked. Plant stall. Route: Kevock Road lies to the south of A678 Loanhead / Lasswade Road

Admission £2.50   Children free.

SATURDAY & SUNDAY 17 & 18 JUNE 2 - 5pm

40% to St Paul's and St George's Project 21 60% net to SGS Charities

---

4. NEWHALL, Carlops   ♿   (Walled Garden only)
(John and Tricia Kennedy)
Traditional 18th century walled garden with huge herbaceous border, shrubberies, fruit and vegetables. Beautiful glen walks along North Esk River. Very young large pond in the process of being planted. Primulas, meconopsis and collection of rosa pimpinellifolia in June, interesting perennials in July, many of which are for sale. Dogs on leads. Route: on A702 Edinburgh/ Biggar, a quarter of a mile after Ninemileburn and a mile before Carlops. Follow signs.
SUNDAY 18 JUNE 11am – 4pm
HOG ROAST, coffee/tea/cake. Large plant stall all home grown.
Admission £2.50 accompanied children free
SUNDAY 9 JULY 5.30 - 8.30pm
Admission £4.00 to include a glass of wine. Large home grown plant stall.
40% William Steel Trust (RBGE) 60% net to SGS Charities

✾ **5. POMATHORN GARDENS, Nr Penicuik**   ♿   (with help on gravel)
A number of gardens varying in size and planting style, situated in farmland 700ft above sea level, all have lovely views over open countryside and the Pentland Hills. The gardens are within walking distance of each other, but visitors with walking difficulties can park or be 'dropped off' at each garden. Teas. Plants. Bric-a-brac and book stalls. Dogs on leads. Route: Pomathorn Road, on B6372, between Penicuik and Howgate, about 5 miles from Ikea and 12 miles from Peebles. Turn onto B6372 from either A701 or B7026 and park at Pomathorn Mill. Admission £2.50 includes all gardens. Children free if accompanied.
SUNDAY 6 AUGUST 2 - 5pm
20% to RNLI   20% to WRVS   60% net to SGS Charities

---

6. ROSECOURT, Inveresk   ♿
(Mr & Mrs G W Burnet)
Small walled garden in the beautiful conservation village of Inveresk. The garden which is open in June (see Inveresk opening under East Lothian) is also open again in December as a winter garden to show that the structure of a garden can be interesting and even attractive. Teas, coffees, soup & sandwiches. Christmas stall & short talks/demonstrations. Route: Inveresk lies to the south of Musselburgh, just off A6124.
Admission £2.50
SUNDAY 3 DECEMBER 11am – 3pm
All to SGS Charities

---

7. THE OLD PARSONAGE and BRAE HOUSE   ♿ (most of garden)
19 & 21 Lugton Brae, Dalkeith
(Mr John Stuart)
The garden was laid out in 1845 with herbaceous borders, shrubs and rose beds and extensive views to the south. The large walled garden grows a wide range of vegetables and fruit with a glasshouse for peaches, vines and figs. Teas. Plant stall. Brae house occupies part of the walled garden with its own flower garden. Route: Lugton is ½ mile north of Dalkeith on east side of A68.
Admission £2.50 Children under 12 free
SUNDAY 11 JUNE 2 - 5.30pm
40% to St Mary's Church Restoration Appeal   60% net to SGS Charities

---

8. THE OLD SUN INN, Newbattle, Dalkeith ♿

(Mr & Mrs J Lochhead)

Small, half acre, garden of island and raised beds containing a collection of species lilies, rock plants and some unusual bulbs - there are also two small interconnecting ponds and a conservatory. Teas possible. Some plants for sale. Route: from Eskbank take B703 (Newtongrange) - garden is immediately opposite entrance to Newbattle Abbey College.

Admission £3.00 Children free

OPEN BY APPOINTMENT (most days) 1 MAY - 30 JULY Tel 0131 663 2648

All to SGS Charities

---

9. SGS 10th ANNIVERSARY PLANT SALE - Joint opening Midlothian & East Lothian held undercover at OXENFOORD FARM, Near Pathhead ♿

Excellent selection of garden and house plants donated from private gardens. Specialist plant stall, run by the NCCPG. Refreshments, home baking, fresh produce. Signed of A68 4 miles south of Dalkeith. Contact telephone number: Mrs Parker 01620 824788 or Mrs Barron 0131 663 1895.

SATURDAY 14 OCTOBER 9am- 2.30pm

40% to Cancer Research UK   60% net to SGS Charities

MORAY & NAIRN

District Organiser: **Mrs J Eckersall,** Knocknagore, Knockando
                 Aberlour on Spey AB38 7SG

Hon. Treasurer: **Dr R Eckersall,** Knocknagore, Knockando
                 Aberlour on Spey AB38 7SG

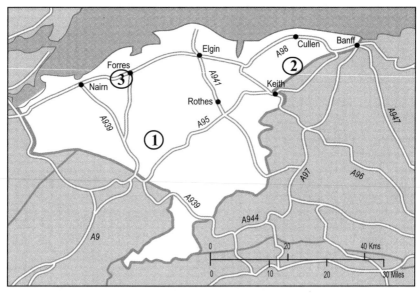

DATES OF OPENING

Knocknagore, Knockando .... By appointment

Knocknagore, Knockando	Sunday 23 April	2 - 5pm
Carestown Steading, Deskford	Sunday 11 June	2 - 5pm
Knocknagore, Knockando	Sunday 23 July	2 - 5pm
Bents Green, 10 Pilmuir Road West, Forres	Sunday 6 August	1.30 - 4.30pm

1. BENTS GREEN, 10 Pilmuir Road West, Forres
(Mrs Lorraine Dingwall)
Small town garden planted in cottage style. formal pond, unusual plants. Interesting varieties of hosta, hardy geraniums and crocosmia. Wide range of plants to buy Route: From centre of Forres take Nairn road, turn left at BP garage into Ramflat Road at end turn into Pilmuir Road then sharp left into Pilmuir Road West.
Admission Adults £2.50 Children free
SUNDAY 6 AUGUST 1.30-4.30pm
40% to Macmillan Cancer Relief 60% net to SGS Charities

2. CARESTOWN STEADING, Deskford, Buckie
(Rora Paglieri)
The best compliment to Carestown garden was paid by The Garden history Society in Scotland when it described it as "Garden history in the making". The garden was started in 1990 and has received accolades from the press, tv and web www.CarestownSteading.com. Every year a new addition is made, the latest being the epitome of the modern vegetable plot which is proving to be a great success: 4 year rotation, raised beds, seeping irrigation. Meanwhile trees and shrubs are maturing, the maze is growing, the ducks are reproducing in the three ponds and the atmosphere is as happy as ever. Not to be forgotten is the 'pearl' of the garden, the courtyard with knot beds and topiary now fully mature.   Teas on the barbecue area by local Guides.
Route: East off B9018 Cullen/Keith (Cullen 3miles, Keith 9½miles). Follow SGS signs towards Milton and Carestown.
Admission £2.50 Children 50p
SUNDAY 11 JUNE 2 - 5pm
All takings to Scotland's Gardens Scheme

3. KNOCKNAGORE, Knockando
(Dr and Mrs Eckersall)
A series of gardens created from rough pasture and moorland since 1995. Comprising trees, herbaceous beds, rockery, courtyard garden and "Sittie Ooterie". Vegetable plot and two ponds, all surrounded by stunning views.   Entrance from 'Cottage Road' which connects the B9102 Archiestown to Knockando road with the Knockando to Dallas road.
Admission Adults £2.50 Children 50p
SUNDAY 23 APRIL 2 - 5pm
An opening in April to give the opportunity to see the spring flowers featuring the daffodils, the entry includes tea and biscuits.
SUNDAY 23 JULY 2 - 5pm - Teas & Plant Stall
Open other times by prior appointment Fax no. 01340 810554
40% to Children's Hospice Association Scotland 60% net to SGS Charities

PERTH & KINROSS

District Organisers: **The Hon Mrs Ranald Noel-Paton**, Pitcurran House,
Abernethy PH2 9LH

Mrs D J W Anstice, Broomhill, Abernethy PH2 9LQ

Area Organisers: **Mrs C Dunphie,** Wester Cloquhat, Bridge of Cally PH10 7JP
Miss L Heriot Maitland, Keepers Cottage, Hill of Errol PH2 7TQ
Mrs M Innes, Kilspindie Manse, Kilspindie PH2 7RX
Lady Livesay, Bute Cottage, Academy Road, Crieff PH7 4AT
Mrs P Mackenzie, Baledmund House, Pitlochry PH16 5RA
Mrs D Nichol, Rossie House, Forgandenny PH2 9EH
Miss Judy Norwell, 20 Pitcullen Terrace, Perth PH2 7EG
Mrs Athel Price, Bolfracks, Aberfeldy PH15 2EX
Miss Bumble Ogilvy Wedderburn, Garden Cottage, Lude,
Blair Atholl, PH18 5TR

Hon. Treasurer: **Mr Cosmo Fairbairn** Alleybank, Bridge of Earn, Perth PH2 9EZ

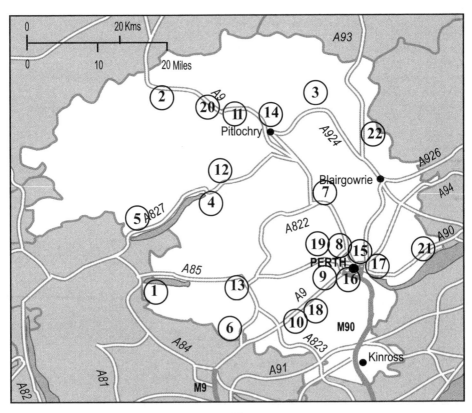

DATES OF OPENING

Ardvorlich, Lochearnhead	7 May to 4 June	All day
Bolfracks, Aberfeldy	1 April - 31October	10am - 6pm
Braco Castle, Braco	1 April - Mid August	10am - 5pm
	October (Wed - Sun)	Other times by Appt.
Cluniemore, Pitlochry	1 May - 1 Oct and	by appointment
Cluny House, Aberfeldy	1 March - 31 October	10am - 6pm
Rossie House, Forgandenny	1 March - 31 October	by appointment
Scone Palace, Perth	1 April - 31 October	9.30 - 5.30pm

Megginch Castle.Errol	Sunday 23 April	2 - 5pm
Glendoick, by Perth	Sunday 7 May	2 - 5pm
Branklyn, Perth	Sunday 7 May	10am - 5pm
Glendoick, by Perth	Sunday 14 May	2 - 5pm
Rossie House, Forgandenny	Sunday 14 May	2 - 6pm
Balnakeilly, Pitlochry	Sunday 21 May	2 - 5.30pm
Cloan, by Auchterarder	Sunday 28 May	10am - 5pm
Bradystone House, Murthly	Sunday 4 June	11am - 4pm
Explorers, The Scottish Plant Hunters Garden, Pitlochry	Sunday 18 June	10am - 5pm
The Cottage, Longforgan	Sunday 25 June	2 - 5pm
Glenearn House, Bridge of Earn	Sunday 2 July	2 - 5.30pm
Strathgarry House, Killiecrankie	Sunday 2 July	2 - 6pm
Wester Cloquhat, Bridge of Cally	Sunday 9 July	2 - 5pm
Auchleeks House, Calvine	Sunday 16 July	2 - 6pm
Boreland, Killin	Sunday 23 July	2 - 5.30pm
Cluniemore, Pitlochry	Sunday 6 August	2 - 5pm
Drummond Castle Gardens, Muthill	Sunday 6 August	1 - 5pm
Cherrybank Gardens, Perth	Sunday 10 September	11am -5pm

1. ARDVORLICH, Lochearnhead
(Mr & Mrs Sandy Stewart)
Beautiful glen with rhododendrons (species and many hybrids) grown in wild conditions amid oaks and birches. Quite steep in places. Gum boots advisable when wet. Dogs on lead please. On South Lochearn Road 3 miles from Lochearnhead, 4½ miles from St Fillans. Probably no access from Lochearnhead.
Admission £3.00 Children under 12 free
7 MAY to 4 JUNE ALL DAY
40% to The Gurkha Welfare Trust 60% net to SGS Charities

2. AUCHLEEKS HOUSE, Calvine
(Mr & Mrs Angus MacDonald)
Auchleeks is a classical Georgian house with a large herbaceous walled garden in a beautiful glen setting, surrounded by hills and mature trees. Teas. Plant stall. Route: North of Blair Atholl turn off A9 at Calvine. B847 towards Kinloch Rannoch, 5 miles on right. Dogs on a lead please
Admission £3.00 Children free
SUNDAY 16 JULY 2 - 6pm
40% to Struan Primary School 60% net to SGS Charities

3. BALNAKEILLY, Pitlochry (If dry)
(Colonel & Mrs Ralph Stewart Wilson)
Mature trees, featuring *Abies procera* (noblis), the 'Noble Fir', originally introduced into Scotland by David Douglas in 1830. These surround a burn and herbaceous borders. Good strolling paths and wonderful views. Dogs on leads please. Teas. Route: From Pitlochry take Kirkmichael Road through Moulin, 400 yards on left past Moulin Hotel.
Admission £3.00
SUNDAY 21 May 2 - 5.30pm
40% to Moulin Hall Trust 60% net to SGS Charities

---

4. BOLFRACKS, Aberfeldy
(The Douglas Hutchison Trust)
Three acre north facing garden with wonderful views overlooking the Tay valley. Burn garden with rhododendrons, azaleas, primulas, meconopsis, etc. in woodland setting. Walled garden with shrubs, herbaceous borders and old fashioned roses. Great selection of bulbs in the spring and good autumn colour with sorbus, gentians and cyclamen. Slippery paths and bridges in wet weather. Not suitable for wheelchairs. Parties, including lunch and teas, available by prior arrangement. Please telephone 01887 820344. No dogs please. Limited range of plants for sale. Route: 2 miles west of Aberfeldy on A827. White gates and Lodge on left.
Admission £3.00 Children under 16 free
1 APRIL - 31 OCTOBER 10am - 6pm
Donation to Scotland's Gardens Scheme

---

5. BORELAND, Killin
(Mrs Angus Stroyan)
A varied garden with borders as the main feature. Very pretty walk along river leading to arboretum. Teas under cover. Plant stall. Route: off A827 through Killin, first turning left over Bridge of Lochay Hotel. House approx. 2 miles on left.
Admission £3.00 Children over 12, 75p
SUNDAY 23 JULY 2 - 5.30pm
40% to Cancer Research UK 60% net to SGS Charities

---

6. BRACO CASTLE, Braco (Partly)
(Mr & Mrs M. van Ballegooijen)
A 19th century landscaped garden comprising woodland and meadow walks with a fine show of spring flowering bulbs, many mature specimen trees and shrubs, with considerable new planting. The partly walled garden is approached on a rhododendron and tree-lined path and features an ornamental pond, extensive hedging and lawns with shrub and herbaceous borders. The planting is enhanced by spectacular views over the castle park to the Ochils. Good autumn colour. Please, no dogs. 1½ mile drive from gates at north end of Braco Village, just west of bridge on A822.
Admission £3.00 Children free
OPEN APRIL - MID AUGUST & OCTOBER, WEDNESDAY - SUNDAY 10 - 5pm
OTHER TIMES BY APPOINTMENT. Please telephone: 01786 880437
40% to The Woodland Trust 60% net to SGS Charities

---

7. BRADYSTONE HOUSE, Murthly ♿ (Partly)
(Mr & Mrs James Lumsden)
True cottage courtyard garden converted ten years ago from derelict farm steading. Ponds, free roaming ducks and hens and many interesting shrubs and ornamental trees. Soup & filled rolls, etc. Plant stall. No dogs please. Route: from south/north follow A9 to Bankfoot, then sign to Murthly. At crossroads in Murthly take private road to Bradystone.
Admission £3.00
SUNDAY 4 JUNE 11am - 4pm
40% to Murthly Village Hall Fund   60% net to SGS Charities

---

8. BRANKLYN, Perth
(The National Trust for Scotland)
This attractive little garden in Perth was once described as "the finest two acres of private garden in the country". It contains an outstanding collection of plants, particularly rhododendrons, alpine, herbaceous and peat-loving plants, which attract gardeners and botanists from all over the world. On A85 Perth/Dundee road. Disabled parking at gate.
Admission £5.00 Concessions £4.00 Family £14.00
SUNDAY 7 MAY 10am - 5pm
40% to The Gardens Fund of The National Trust for Scotland   60% net to SGS Charities

---

✿ 9. CHERRYBANK GARDENS, Perth ♿
Cherrybank Gardens and Visitor Centre has over 50,000 plants and over 900 varieties of heather, the UK's largest collection. It is a stunning 6 acre garden and is designed to provide a rich mix of colour throughout the year. It also plays an important conservationist role. All this is complemented by artworks, and water features including an acoustic pool and trout stream. Soup & rolls/ teas & coffee are available in the café. Plants for sale. Gift Shop. Guide dogs only, please. All disabled facilities and tarmac paths. Open 7 days a week, March - December, 01738 472800. Route: Entrance on Necessity Brae just off A93, Glasgow Road, up hill and past the Bank on right.
Admission £3.75 Concessions £3.40 Children (12-16) £2.50 Children under 12 free.
SUNDAY 10 SEPTEMBER 11am - 5pm
40% to Scotland's Gardens Trust   60% net to SGS Charities

---

10. CLOAN, by Auchterarder ♿ (partly)
(Mr & Mrs Richard Haldane)
Gardens and policies extending to roughly 7 acres, originally laid out in the 1850s. Mature trees, rhododendrons and azaleas. Walled, water and wild gardens and delightful woodland walks. Peacocks - so no dogs please. Soup/teas Route: south out of Auchterarder (Abbey Road) then follow yellow signs.
Admission £3.00 Children (under 16) 50p
SUNDAY 28 MAY 10 - 5pm
40% to Friends of St Margaret's 60% net to SGS Charities

---

11. CLUNIEMORE, Pitlochry   ♿

(Major Sir David & Lady Butter)

Mature garden in a beautiful setting surrounded by hills. Rock and water gardens, lawns, herbaceous and annual border. Roses, shrubs and a short (signed) woodland walk above the garden. Greenhouses. Plant stall. Teas, biscuits and ice cream. On A9 Pitlochry bypass.
Admission £3.00 Children under 16 free

SUNDAY 6 AUGUST 2 - 5pm

Also open by appointment 1 MAY - 1 OCTOBER Please telephone: 01796 472006

40% to The Pushkin Prizes in Scotland 60% net to SGS Charities

---

12. CLUNY HOUSE, Aberfeldy

(Mr J & Mrs W Mattingley)

A wonderful, wild woodland garden overlooking the scenic Strathtay valley. Experience the grandeur of one of Britain's widest trees, the complex leaf variation of the Japanese maple, the beauty of the American trillium, or the diversity of Asiatic primulas. A treasure not to be missed. No dogs please. Route: 3½ miles from Aberfeldy on Weem to Strathtay Road.
Admission £3.50 Children under 16 free

1 MARCH - 31 OCTOBER 10am - 6pm

Donation to Scotland's Gardens Scheme

---

13. DRUMMOND CASTLE GARDENS, Crieff   ♿

(Grimsthorpe & Drummond Castle Trust Ltd)

The Gardens of Drummond Castle were originally laid out in 1630 by John Drummond, 2nd Earl of Perth. In 1830 the parterre was changed to an Italian style. One of the most interesting features is the multi-faceted sundial designed by John Mylne, Master Mason to Charles I. The formal garden is said to be one of the finest in Europe and is the largest of its type in Scotland. Open daily May to October 2 – 6 pm (last entrance 5 pm). Entrance 2 miles south of Crieff on Muthill road (A822).
Admission £3.00 OAPs £2.00 Children £1.00 Teas, raffle, entertainments & stalls.

SUNDAY 6 AUGUST 1 - 5pm

40% to British Limbless Ex-Servicemen's Association 60% net to SGS Charities

---

14. EXPLORERS, The Scottish Plant Hunters Garden, Pitlochry   ♿

A wonderful new garden overlooking the River Tummel. Planted with a mixture of species and cultivars to represent The Scottish Plant Collectors. Teas at Theatre. Plant Stall. Route: A9 to Pitlochry town, follow signs to Pitlochry Festival Theatre.
Admission £3.00 Children £1.00

SUNDAY 18 JUNE 10am - 5pm

40% to Acting for Others 60% net to SGS Charities

Why not look up the gardens on our website?
www.gardensofscotland.org
PHOTOS AND MAPS

15. GLENDOICK, by Perth ♿ (Only garden by house)
(Peter, Patricia, Kenneth & Jane Cox)
Glendoick was recently included in the Independent on Sunday's exclusive survey of Europe's top 50 gardens and boasts a unique collection of plants collected by 3 generations of Coxes from their plant-hunting expeditions to China and the Himalayas. Fine collection of rhododendrons, azaleas, primula, meconopsis, kalmia and sorbus in the enchanting woodland garden with naturalised wild flowers. Extensive peat garden, nursery and hybrid trial garden. No dogs please. Meals and snacks available at Glendoick Garden Centre. Route: follow signs to Glendoick Garden Centre off A90 Perth - Dundee road.
Admission £3.00 School age children free
SUNDAYS 7 & 14 MAY 2 - 5pm
Donation to Scotland's Gardens Scheme and WWF

⊛ 16. GLENEARN HOUSE, Bridge of Earn
(Mr and Mrs Hans-Jurgen Queisser)
Regency house (not open) in lovely setting, surrounded by park and woodlands with walks to a fine recently planted walled garden. Also a charming small loch beside the restored mid-17th century fortified house, Ecclesiamagirdle, and its chapel and burial ground. Teas and Plant Stall. No dogs please. Route: Exit 9 from M90 into Bridge of Earn. Take B935 (Forgandenny Road) for 1 mile, left to Pitkeathly Wells, then ¾ mile to Glenearn gates on right.
Admission £3.00 Children (under 16 years) free.
SUNDAY 2 JULY 2 - 5.30pm
40% to Rachel House, Kinross   60% net to SGS Charities

---

17. MEGGINCH CASTLE, Errol ♿
(Captain Humphrey Drummond & Mr Giles & Hon Mrs Herdman)
15th century turreted castle (not open) with Gothic courtyard and pagoda dovecote. 1,000 year old yews and topiary. Astrological garden. Daffodils and rhododendrons. Water garden. On A90 between Perth (9½ miles) and Dundee (12 miles) south side of road. Refreshments.
Admission £3.00 Children free
SUNDAY 23 APRIL 2 - 5pm
40% to All Saints Church, Glencarse   60% net to SGS Charities

---

18. ROSSIE HOUSE, Forgandenny ♿ (partly)
(Mr and Mrs David B Nichol)
This mature woodland garden, with undulating terrain and including a water garden and a walled garden, provides year round interest. In early spring snowdrops and aconites abound, while through May a carpet of bluebells underplant towering rhododendrons, specimen trees, cornuses, a 30 foot davidia involucrata and the fragrant magnolia hypoleuca. A stewartia flowers in July and there are huge lacecap hydrangeas and eucryphias in August and September, followed by intense autumn colours. Sculptures by David Annand and Nigel Ross. Cream teas and Plant Stall. Dogs on leads please. Forgandenny is on the B935, between Bridge of Earn and Dunning.
Admission £3.00 Children £1.00
SUNDAY 14 MAY 2 - 6pm
40% to Forgandenny Village Hall Fund   60% net to SGS Charities
ALSO OPEN BY APPOINTMENT 1 March - 31 October. Please telephone: 01738 812265
40% to Sandpiper Trust   60% net to SGS Charities

---

19. SCONE PALACE, Perth ♿

(The Earl & Countess of Mansfield)

Extensive and well laid out grounds and a magnificent pinetum dating from 1848; there is a Douglas fir raised from the original seed sent from America in 1824. The woodland garden has attractive walks amongst the rhododendrons and azaleas and leads into the Monks' Playgreen and Friar's Den of the former Abbey of Scone. Murray Star beech maze. Route A93. Perth 2 miles
Admission (Grounds only) £3.80 Students & OAPs £3.50 Children £2.50

1 APRIL - 31 OCTOBER 9.30am - 5.30pm (last entry 5pm)

Donation to Scotland's Gardens Scheme

---

20. STRATHGARRY HOUSE, Killiecrankie ♿

(Mr & Mrs S Thewes)

Early 19th century walled garden laid out in a cruciform and set in beautiful surroundings. A large collection of apple trees, some of which are presently unknown, others are rare, old Scottish varieties and are underplanted with large herbaceous borders. Raised vegetable garden and small courtyard garden also with raised borders.
Teas. Plant stall. Route: Between Pitlochry-Blair Atholl, off the old A9 at Killiecrankie.
Admission £3.00 Children under 16 Free

SUNDAY 2 JULY 2 - 6pm

20% to Anthony Nolan Bone Marrow Trust 20 % to Kilmaveonaig Church 60% net to SGS Charities

---

21. THE COTTAGE, Main Street, Longforgan ♿

(Dr and Mrs Andrew Reid)

This 2 acre garden faces south and has views of the Tay and Fife Hills. It is designed for year round interest with rhododendron and azalea beds, herbaceous borders and roses. There are water features and many interesting trees including an historic silver birch. Situated in the middle of Longforgan. Teas. Plant stall. No dogs please. Street parking. Route: take Longforgan turning off A90 between Perth (15 miles) and Dundee (5 miles)
Admission £3.00 Children 50p

SUNDAY 25 JUNE 2 - 5pm

40% to Barnardo's 60% net to SGS Charities

---

22. WESTER CLOQUHAT, Bridge of Cally

(Brigadier & Mrs Christopher Dunphie)

Small garden enlarged in 2001 to include a water garden. Lawns, mixed borders with a wide range of shrubs, roses and herbaceous plants. Splendid situation with fine view down to the River Ericht. Teas and plant stall. No dogs please. Route: turn off A93 just north of Bridge of Cally and follow signs for ½ mile.
Admission £3.00 Children under 16 free

SUNDAY 9 JULY 2 - 5pm

40% to Royal Scottish National Orchestra 60% net to SGS Charities

---

Why not look up the gardens on our website?
www.gardensofscotland.org
PHOTOS AND MAPS

RENFREW & INVERCLYDE

Joint District Organisers: **Mrs J R Hutton,** Auchenclava, Finlaystone, Langbank PA14 6TJ

Mrs Daphne Ogg, Nittingshill, Kilmacolm PA13 4SG

Area Organisers: **Lady Denholm,** Newton of Bell Trees, Lochwinnoch PA12 4JL

Mrs Rosemary Leslie, High Mathernock Farm, Auchentiber Road, Kilmalcolm.

Mr J A Wardrop DL, St Kevins, Victoria Road, PaisleyPA2 9PT

PR - **Mrs G West,** Woodlands, 2 Birchwood Road, Uplawmoor,G78 4DG

Hon. Treasurer: **Mrs Jean Gillan,** Bogriggs Cottage, Carlung, West Kilbride KA23 9PS

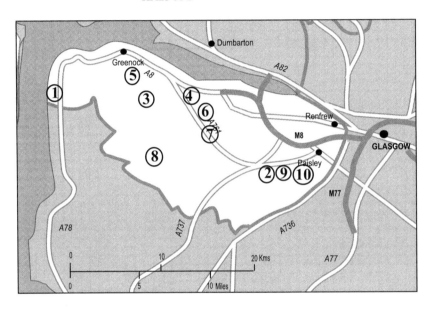

DATES OF OPENING

Ardgowan, Inverkip	Sunday 19 February	2 - 5pm
Finlaystone, Langbank	Sunday 9 April	2 - 5pm
Paisley, Park Road Gardens	Sunday 21 May	2 - 5pm
Carruth, Bridge of Weir	Sunday 4 June	2 - 5pm
Sma Shot Cottages Heritage Centre, Paisley	Wednesday 14 June	12 - 4pm
Lochwinnoch Gardens.	Sunday 25 June	2 - 5pm
Johnstone Gardens. .	Sunday 2 July	2 - 5pm
Houston Gardens.	Sunday 9 July	2 - 5pm
Sma Shot Cottages Heritage Cente, Paisley	Saturday 15 July	12 - 4pm
Greenoch West Gardens.	Sunday 30 July	2 - 5pm
Barshaw Park, Paisley	Sunday 6 August	2 - 5pm
SGS Plant Sale, Finlaystone, Langbank	Sunday 10 September	11.30am - 4pm

1. ARDGOWAN, Inverkip ♿ (not advisable if wet)
(Lady Shaw Stewart)
Woodland walks carpeted with snowdrops. (Strong waterproof footwear advised.) Tea in house. Snowdrop and plant stall, tombola and home produce. Inverkip 1½ miles. Glasgow/Largs buses to and from Inverkip Village
Admission: £2.00 Children under 10 free
SUNDAY 19 FEBRUARY 2 - 5pm
40% to Ardgowan Hospice   60% net to SGS Charities

---

2. BARSHAW PARK - Walled Garden, Paisley ♿ (gravel paths)
(Environmental Services Department, Renfrewshire Council)
Walled garden displaying a varied selection of plants, some of which are suitable for the blind to smell and feel. These would include a colourful layout of summer bedding plants, herbaceous borders, mixed shrub borders and rose beds. Teas and Plant Stall. Route: from Paisley town centre along the Glasgow road (A737) pass Barshaw Park and take first left into Oldhall Road & then first left again into walled garden car park. Pedestrian visitors can approach from Barshaw Park.
Admission by donation
SUNDAY 6 AUGUST 2 - 5pm
40% to Erskine Hospital   60% net to SGS Charities

---

3. CARRUTH, Bridge of Weir
(Mr & Mrs Charles Maclean)
Large Plant Sale including a wide selection of herbaceous, herbs, shrubs etc. Over 20 acres of long established rhododendrons, woodland and lawn gardens in lovely landscaped setting.Young arboretum.   Home made teas. Access from B786 Kilmacolm/Lochwinnoch road or from Bridge of Weir via Torr Road.
Admission £3.00
SUNDAY 4 JUNE 2 - 5pm
40% to Mariè Curie Cancer Care 60% net to SGS Charities

---

4. FINLAYSTONE, Langbank ♿
(Mr & Mrs Arthur MacMillan)
Historic connection with John Knox and Robert Burns. Richly varied gardens with unusual plants overlooking the Clyde. A profusion of daffodils and early rhododendrons. Waterfalls & pond. Woodland walks with imaginative play and picnic areas. "Eye-opener" centre with shop. Doll Museum. Ranger service. Plant stall. Teas in the Celtic Tree in the walled garden.
Website: www.finlaystone.co.uk
On A8 west of Langbank, 10 minutes by car west of Glasgow Airport.
Admission £3.50 Children (under 4 free) & OAPs £2.50
SUNDAY 9 APRIL 2 - 5pm
40% to Quarrier's Village   60% net to SGS Charities
SUNDAY 10 SEPTEMBER SGS Special Plant Sale 11.30am - 4pm
An opportunity to purchase plants at the end of season clearance sale. Finlaystone gardens and woodlands will be open as usual on this day.
40% of plant sales to Rokba UK Overseas Project. 60% net to SGS Charities

---

❀ 5. GREENOCK WEST GARDENS

St Margaret's Church, Finch Road
Colourful church garden maintained by volunteers. Teas. Plant Stall. Directions: from Inverkip Road take Gateside Avenue/Grieve Road then turn left at Holy Cross School into Finch Road.

Lady Alice Primary School, Inverkip Road
An empty courtyard transformed by the pupils into an imaginative award-winning garden. Plant Stall. Directions: A78 Greenock/Inverkip Road.

9 Battery Park Avenue
(Mr & Mrs Mitchell)
The garden has a large driveway with raised beds on both sides which are filled with a variety of shrubs and bedding plants. The back garden is paved and again has raised bed with trees, shrubs & herbaceous plants. Plant Stall. Directions: Just east of Battery Park. Main Road Greenock/ Gourock

"La Casita", 21 Finnart Road
(Mr & Mrs J Thompson)
Small walled south-facing garden with lawn, flower borders, water features and a large variety of containers. Plant Stall. Directions: turn into Campbell Street from Brougham Street (A770) at traffic lights/ McMillan Motors turn left into Finnart Road at top of hill beyond Ardgown School and Newton Street.

Admission £3.00
SUNDAY 30 JULY 2 - 5pm
40% shared by St Margaret's Church, Children 1st, Imperial Cancer Research & Ardgowan Hospice. 60% net to SGS Charities

---

6. HOUSTON GARDENS   ♿ (with assistance)

Old Schoolhouse
(Miss Jean Dawson)
A mature garden of about one third of an acre: comprising herbaceous plants, grasses and acers. Access via gate on Main Street between Houston Inn and War Memorial.

Woodlands Cottage - wheelchair friendly
(Hamish and Mary McKelvie)
This is a secluded garden situated within the woods of Houston Estate containing a selection of shrubs and herbaceous plants including many hostas and ferns. There are also 3 glasshouses accomodating a large selection of prizewinning cacti and succulents.

Barochan West Lodge
(Alistair and Anne Cleland)
Three quarter acre terraced garden has a selection of conifers, herbaceious borders and shrubs. A small pond on top and bottom level. Sunken garden on site of Comlie Cottage demolished 1891. Front garden: mature trees and rockery.

Teas at Houston and Killellan church hall in village centre. Plant stall at Woodlands Cottage. Gardens will be well signposted. Extreme care required on side roads.

Admission £3.00   Children under 10 free
SUNDAY 9 JULY 2 - 5pm
40% shared by Multiple Sclerosis, St Vincents Hospice - Johnstone Accord Hospice - Paisley and CHAS   60% net to SGS Charities

---

7. JOHNSTONE GARDENS

Five well tended gardens each quite distinctive with much to interest the visitor:

1. **23 Hagg Road** (Yvonne and Jim Morris)
2. **20 Hagg Road** (Betty Logue)
3. **11 Hagg Road** (Danny and Joan McLaughlin)
4. **10 Bevan Grove** (John and Agnes Kenny)
5. **44 Hagg Crescent** (Ted & Betty Palmer)

Teas at 20 Hagg Road - Plant stall.

From High Street turn west into McDowall Street heading for Kilbarchan. Take north turn into Hagg Road at Graham Street / Kilbarchan Road junction. Well signposted thereafter.

Admission £3.00

SUNDAY 2 JULY 2 - 5pm

40% St. Vincent's Hospice   60% net to SGS Charities

---

8. LOCHWINNOCH GARDENS

CATHCART COTTAGE, 36 Calder Street (Anne & Gordon Nicholl)

Walled garden stretching back from old cottage (1838) containing an astonishing selection of plants.

23 Main Street (Jenny & Zul Bhatia)

A plantsman's garden with a wide variety of mostly perennials, including many rare and scarce plants.

Lochwinnoch Sustainable Garden

Behind Parish Church, Church Street

Recently completed garden for community use, highlighting recycling and composting (including wormery), as well as a variety of planting to attract wildlife.

RSPB Nature Reserve, Largs Road, Lochwinnoch

Small garden with variety of plants beneficial to wildlife. Teas and plant stall at this location. Additionally a group of small village gardens will be open. Route: on A760 Johnstone to Largs Road, look for yellow signs. Maps will be available.

Admission £3.00 Children free (Includes RSPB hides and trails)

SUNDAY 25 JUNE 2 - 5pm

40% shared between Chest, Heart & Stroke Scotland & Amani Centre for Children (Tanzania) 60% net to SGS Charities

---

9. PAISLEY, PARK ROAD GARDENS

24 Park Road

(Douglas & Pamela Smith)

A large mature garden surrounding the late Victorian sandstone villa 'Bushes House' dating from 1896. The garden features large lawns, mature trees and conifers complemented by a wide range of colourful shrubs and perennials.

26 Park Road

(Barrie & Lesley Scholefield)

Described on a previous opening in 2002 as a new 5 year old garden, the garden has developed further with a maturing selection of trees, conifers, large shrubs, formal and informal lawns, a bog garden and a vegetable garden all set within the framework of mature trees formerly the front garden off number 24 Park Road. Recent additions are a deck/out-door room, formal parterehedging to the vegetable plot and a variety of pavings.

'Scotscraig'   (limited)

(Susan Fleming)

Restoration of this magnificent Edwardian house is almost complete after many years dedication by the family. Guided viewing to the house will be allowed by donation. The house sits in mature gardens featuring lawns, terraced beds and a wildlife pond. Route: Proceed south by Causeyside Street from ring road at Canal Street. Calside is main route to Glennifer Braes. Park Road is reached from Calside by steep hills.

Admission £2.50 to cover all three gardens. Children under 10 free.

Home baked teas at no. 26. Plant stall at no. 24.

SUNDAY 21 MAY 2 - 5pm

40% to Accord Hospice   60% net to SGS Charities

❀ 10. SMA' SHOT COTTAGES HERITAGE CENTRE, Paisley

(Old Paisley Society)

Small enclosed courtyard garden. Enjoy the 19th Century weaver's garden designed to celebrate the 21st anniversary of Sma' Shot Cottages. All plants are true to the period. Assistance in the creation of the garden was provided by the Beechgrove gardeners. Visitors may also see the rare "Paisley Gem" (Dianthus) and the new "Viola Sma' Shot Cottages" bred by local gardener, Hugh Boyd. Plant stall. Home baked teas. Route: off New Street in Paisley Town Centre.

Admission free but donations to SGS appreciated.

WEDNESDAY 14 JUNE - SATURDAY 15 JULY 12 - 4pm

ROSS, CROMARTY, SKYE & INVERNESS

District Organiser: **Lady Lister-Kaye,** House of Aigas, Beauly IV4 7AD

Hon. Treasurer: **Mr Kenneth Haselock,** 2 Tomich, Strathglass, by Beauly IV4 7LZ

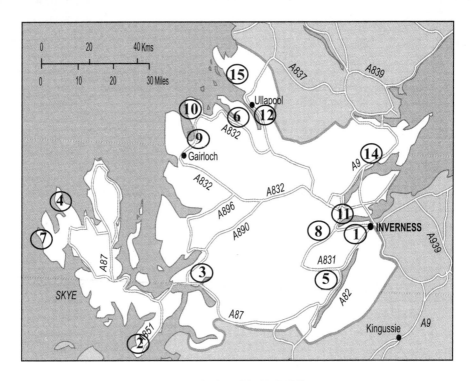

DATES OF OPENING

Abriachan, Loch Ness Side .... February - November   9am - dusk
An Acarsaid, Ord, Isle of Skye .... April - October   10am - 5.30pm
Attadale, Strathcarron .... 1 Apr - end Oct Closed Suns   10am - 5.30pm
Balmeanach House, Struan .... Weds & Sats end Apr - mid Oct 11am - 4.30pm
Coiltie Garden, Divach, Drumnadrochit .... By Appt & 17 June - 23 July   Noon - 7pm
Dunvegan Castle, Isle of Skye .... 21 Mar- 31 Oct Mon - Sun   10am - 5.30pm
Leathad Ard, Isle of Lewis .... Tues, Thurs, Sats 10 Jun-26 Aug   2 - 6pm
Leckmelm Shrubbery & Arboretum .... 1 April - 31 October   10am - 6pm
The Hydroponicum, Achiltibuie .... 3 Apr - 30 Sep & Mon - Fri in Oct   10 - 6pm

Dundonnell House, Dundonnel, Wester Ross .... Thursday 6 Apil   2 - 5pm
Inverewe, Poolewe .... Saturday 15 April   9.30am - 5pm
Kilcoy Castle, Muir of Ord .... Sunday 14 May   2 - 6pm
The Hydroponicum, Achiltibuie .... Sunday 14 May   10am - 6pm
House of Gruinard, by Laide .... Wednesday 31 May   2 - 5pm
Attadale, Strathcarron .... Saturday 3 June   2 - 5pm
Dundonnell House, Dundonnel, Wester Ross .... Wednesday 7 June   2 - 5pm
House of Aigas & Field Centre, By Beauly .... Sunday 25 June   2 - 5.30pm
Kilcoy Castle, Muir of Ord .... Sunday 2 July   2 - 6pm
Novar, Evanton .... Sunday 9 July   2.30pm
House of Aigas & Field Centre, By Beauly .... Sunday 23 July   2 - 5.30pm
Dundonnell House, Dundonnel, Wester Ross .... Thursday 17 August   2 - 5pm
The Hydroponicum, Achiltibuie .... Sunday 20 August   10am - 6pm
Inverewe, Poolewe .... Sunday 10 September   9.30am - 5pm

1. ABRIACHAN GARDEN NURSERY, Loch Ness Side

(Mr & Mrs Davidson)

An outstanding garden. Over 4 acres of exciting plantings, with winding paths through native woodlands. Seasonal highlights – hellebores, primulas, meconopsis, hardy geraniums and colour-themed summer beds. Views over Loch Ness. New path to pond through the Bluebell Wood.

Admission £2.00.

FEBRUARY to NOVEMBER 9am - dusk

Donation to Scotland's Gardens Scheme

---

2. AN ACARSAID, Ord, Sleat, Isle of Skye

(Mrs Eileen MacInnes)

A two acre garden perched on low cliffs above the shore of Loch Eishort with stunning views to the Cuillins. Informal mixed plantings, started in the 1960s, with shrubbery and viewpoint, lawns, borders and scree bed and many cobbled paths. Route: Take A851 from Broadford or Armadale. Ord is signposted 5 miles from Armadale.

Admission by donation box.

APRIL - OCTOBER 10am - 5.30pm

Donation to Crossroads Care & SGS Charities

---

3. ATTADALE, Strathcarron   ♿ (partial)

(Mr & Mrs Ewen Macpherson)

The Gulf Stream and surrounding hills and rocky cliffs create a microclimate for outstanding water gardens, old rhododendrons, unusual trees and fern collection in a geodesic dome. Japanese garden. Plants for sale. Tea room. On A890 between Strathcarron and South Strome.

Admission £3.00 Children £1.00   ♿ free

1 APRIL - end OCTOBER 10am - 5.30pm Closed Sundays

Donation to Scotland's Gardens Scheme

SATURDAY 3 JUNE 2 - 5pm Teas in house. Plant stall.

40% to The Howard Doris Centre 60% to SGS Charities

---

4. BALMEANACH HOUSE, Struan, Isle of Skye

(Mrs Arlene Macphie)

A formal garden with herbaceous border and bedding: and an azalea/rhododendron walk. To make this garden one third of an acre of croft land was fenced in during the late 1980s and there is now a woodland dell with fairies, three ponds and a shrubbery. Teas and Plant Stall. Route: A87 to Sligachan, turn left, Balmeanach is 5 miles north of Struan and 5 miles south of Dunvegan.

Admission By donation box - suggested donation - £2.00

WEDNESDAY & SATURDAYS END - APRIL - MID OCTOBER 11am - 4.30pm

40% to SSPCA 60% net to SGS Charities

5. COILTIE GARDEN, Divach, Drumnadrochit ♿

(Gillian & David Nelson)
A wooded garden, an amalgamation of a Victorian flower garden abandoned 60 years ago and a walled field with a large moraine. This garden has been made over the past 20 years and development work is still in progress. Many trees, old and new, mixed shrub and herbaceous borders, roses, wall beds, rockery. No dogs please. Off A82 at Drumnadrochit. Take road signposted Divach uphill 2 miles. Past Divach Lodge, 150m.
Admission £2.00 Children free
OPEN DAILY JUNE 17 - JULY 23 Noon - 7pm or by appointment tel: 01456 450219
40% to Amnesty International   60% to SGS Charities

---

6. DUNDONNELL HOUSE, Dundonnell, Wester Ross ♿ (partially)

Camelias and magnolias and bulbs in spring, rhodedendrons, and laburnum walk in this ancient walled garden. Delightful new borders for all year colour, centred around one of the oldest yews in Scotland. Riverside walks below the peaks of An Teallach in the fine arboretum. Restored Victorian glasshouse compliments the specime holly and tulip trees. No dogs please. (Maggie's Tea Room for teas - 4 miles towards Little Loch Broom). Route: off A832 between Braemore and Gairloch. Take Badralloch turn for 1 mile.
THURSDAY 6 APRIL 2 - 5pm - No teas.
WEDNESDAY 7 JUNE 2 - 5.30pm - Teas (Maggie's Tea Room, 4 miles towards Little Loch Broom)
THURSDAY 17 AUGUST 2 - 5.30pm - No teas.
40% to Maggie's Centre 60% net to SGS Charities

---

7. DUNVEGAN CASTLE, Isle of Skye

Dating from the 13th century and continuously inhabited by the Chiefs of MacLeod, this romantic fortress stronghold occupies a magnificent lochside setting. The gardens, originally laid out in the 18th century, have been extensively replanted and inlcude lochside walks, woodlands and water gardens and a walled garden. Licensed restaurant. Two craft shops, woollen shop, kilts and country wear shop, clan exhibition, audio-visual theatre. Pedigree Highland cattle fold, boat trips to seal colony. Route: Dunvegan Village 1 mile, 23 miles west of Portree.
Admission to Castle and Gardens: Adults £7.00, OAPs/Students & groups £6.00 Children (5-15) £4.00
Admission to Gardens only: Adults £5.00, OAPs and Students £3.50, Children £3.00
21 MARCH - 31 OCTOBER Mon - Sun 10am - 5.30pm (last entry 5pm)
Castle & Gardens November to Mid March, Mon - Sun 11am - 5.30pm (last entry 3.30pm)
Donation to Scotland's Gardens Scheme

---

8. HOUSE of AIGAS and FIELD CENTRE, by Beauly

(Sir John and Lady Lister-Kaye)
Aigas has a woodland walk overlooking the Beauly River with a collection of named Victorian specimen trees now being restored and extended with a garden of rockeries, herbaceous borders and shrubberies. Home made teas in house. Guided walks on nature trails. Route 4½ miles from Beauly on A831 Cannich/Glen Affric road. No dogs please.
Admission from £3.00 Children free
SUNDAY'S 25 JUNE & 23 JULY 2 - 5.30pm
40% to Highland Hospice   60% net to SGS Charities

---

9. HOUSE OF GRUINARD, by Laide
(The Hon Mrs A G Maclay)
Hidden and unexpected garden developed in sympathy with stunning west coast estuary location. Wide variety of herbaceous and shrub borders with water garden and extended wild planting. Large choice of plants for sale. On A832 12 miles north of Inverewe and 9 miles south of Dundonnell. Teas.
Admission £2.50 Children under 16 free
WEDNESDAY 31 MAY 2 - 5pm
40% to Highland Hospice   60% net to SGS Charities

---

10. INVEREWE, Poolewe &
(The National Trust for Scotland)
Magnificent 50-acre Highland garden, surrounded by mountains, moorland and sea-loch. Founded from 1862 by Osgood Mackenzie, it now includes a wealth of exotic plants, from Australian tree ferns to Chinese rhododendrons to South African bulbs. Shop and self-service restaurant. Plant sales.
Admission £8.00   (For further price information / concessions please see NTS advert at back of book)
SATURDAY 15 APRIL & SUNDAY 10 SEPTEMBER 9.30am - 5pm
40% to The Gardens Fund of the National Trust for Scotland   60% net to SGS Charities

---

11. KILCOY CASTLE, Muir of Ord   &
(Mr & Mrs Nick McAndrew)
16th century castle (not open) surrounded by extensive terraced lawns, walled garden with fine herbaceous and shrub borders, surrounding vegetable garden. Woodland areas with rhododendrons, azaleas and particularly fine mature trees and shrubs. Winner of "Inverness Courier" 'Large garden of the Year' award 2001, 2002 and 2005. Route: A9 to Tore roundabout, A832 signed Beauly and Muir of Ord. After 1½ miles, turn right at church signed Kilcoy, entrance is ½ mile on left.
Admission £2.50 Children under 12 free
SUNDAYS 14 MAY & 2 JULY 2 - 6pm
40% to Highland Hospice   60% net to SGS Charities

---

12. LECKMELM SHRUBBERY & ARBORETUM, by Ullapool
(Mr & Mrs Peter Troughton)
The restored 12 acre arboretum, planted in the 1870s, is full of splendid and rare trees, including 2 "Champions", specie rhododendrons, azaleas and shrubs. Warmed by the Gulf Stream, this tranquil woodland garden has alpines, meconopsis, palms, bamboos and winding paths which lead down to the sea.
Parking in walled garden.Situated by the shore of Loch Broom 3 miles south of Ullapool on the A835 Inverness/Ullapool road.
Admission £2.50 Children under 16 free
OPEN DAILY 1 APRIL - 31 OCTOBER 10am - 6pm
Donation to Scotland's Gardens Scheme and Local Charities

---

13. LEATHAD ARD, Upper Carloway, Isle of Lewis
(Rowena & Stuart Oakley)
A sloping garden view towards East Loch Roag. The garden has evolved as the shelter hedges have grown, dividing the garden into separate areas with bog gardens, herbaceious borders, cutting borders, patio and vegetables. Route: take A858 from Shawbost to Carloway. First right after entering village (opposite football pitch). First house on right.
Donations welcome
TUESDAY'S, THURSDAY'S AND SATURDAY'S 10 JUNE TO 26 AUGUST 2 - 6pm
40% to Red Cross   60% net to SGS Charities

14. NOVAR, Evanton   ♿ (most areas)
(Mr & Mrs Ronald Munro Ferguson)
Water gardens with flowering shrubs, trees and plants, especially rhododendrons and azaleas. Large, five acre walled garden with formal 18th century oval pond (restored). New plantings since last year. Teas. Plant stall. Off B817 between Evanton and junction with A836; turn west up Novar Drive.
Admission £2.50 Children free
SUNDAY 9 JULY 2.30pm
40% to Diabetes Charities   60% net to SGS Charities

15. THE HYDROPONICUM, Achiltibuie   ♿ (lower level)
(The Rt Hon Viscount Gough)
Situated as far north as Alaska, this pioneering indoor garden, overlooks the beautiful Summer Isles. Personally guided tours of modern growing houses show a magnificent array of flowers, fruits, vegetables and herbs growing in 3 different climatic zones without either soil or pesticides. Hourly guided tours. Sunshine Room - a hands-on energy exhibition. Gift shop. Lilypond Café. Children's activities. Plant sales. Mail Order. Please note: our 3 growing houses are all on the lower level. Route: turn off A835 on to single track road to Achiltibuie and follow signs.
Admission £5.50 Children £3.50 Concessions £4.50 Family ticket £16.00
SUNDAYS 14 MAY AND 20 AUGUST 10am - 6pm
40% to R N L I   60% net to SGS Charities
Garden also open daily 3 April - 30 September
October Monday - Friday 11.30am - 3.30pm Tours at 12pm & 2pm.
For further opening details see advert on page 131

ROXBURGH

District Organiser: **Mrs M D Blacklock,** Stable House, Maxton, St Boswells TD6 0EX

Area Organiser: **Mrs T R Harley**, Estate House, Smailholm TD5 7PH

Hon Treasurer: **Mr Peter Jeary,** Kalemouth, Eckford, Kelso

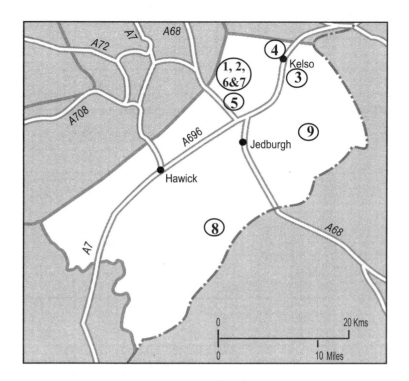

DATES OF OPENING

Floors Castle, Kelso .... Open daily all year.
Monteviot House, Jedburgh .... Open daily 1 April - 31 October   12 - 5pm

Benrig, Benrig Cottage & Stable House. .... Sunday 2 July   2 - 6pm
Floors Castle, Kelso - Gardeners' Festival .... Sat & Sun 8 & 9 July
Corbet Tower, Morebattle .... Sunday 16 July   2 - 6pm
West Leas, Bonchester Bridge .... Sunday 23 July   2 - 6pm
St. Boswells Village. .... Sunday 30 July   2 - 6pm
Yetholm Village .... Sunday 6 August   2 - 6pm

1. BENRIG, St Boswells
(Mr & Mrs Nigel Houldsworth)
The garden at Benrig lies above the Tweed with fabulous views. In a semi-walled area, the
skilled use of shrub roses and herbaceous plants create a tranquil atmosphere. The woodland
walk is planted with interesting young trees and shrubs against a background of mature trees.
Dogs on leads please. Route: two minutes from A68 on the A699 to Kelso.
JOINT OPENING WITH BENRIG COTTAGE & STABLE HOUSE situated on the same road.
Admission £3.00 for all 3 gardens. Children free.
SUNDAY 2 JULY 2 - 6pm
40% to Mertoun & Maxton Church Fund 60% net to SGS Charities

2. BENRIG COTTAGE, St Boswells &

(Mrs H.H. Houldsworth)

This cottage garden is filled with shrub roses, herbaceous and alpine plants. Two small ponds with connecting rill, and a shrub border make this the most charming and congenial space. Dogs on lead please. Route: two minutes from A68 on the A699 to Kelso.

JOINT OPENING WITH BENRIG & STABLE HOUSE, situated on the same road.

Admission £3.00 for all 3 gardens. Children free.

SUNDAY 2 JULY 2 - 6pm

40% to Mertoun & Maxton Church Fund 60% net to SGS Charities

---

3. CORBET TOWER, Morebattle & (partially)

(Simon & Bridget Fraser)

Scottish Victorian garden set in parklands in the foothills of the Cheviots. The garden includes formal parterre with old fashioned roses, well stocked traditional walled garden and attractive woodland walk. Teas. Route: from A68 north of Jedburgh take A698 for Kelso. At Kalemouth follow B6401 to Morebattle then road marked Hownam to Corbet Tower.

Admission £3.00 Children over 12 £1.50

SUNDAY 16 JULY 2 - 6PM

40% to Children's Society 60% net to SGS Charities

---

4. FLOORS CASTLE, Kelso &

(The Duke of Roxburghe)

The largest inhabited house in Scotland enjoys glorious views across parkland, the River Tweed & the Cheviot Hills. Woodland garden, riverside and woodland walks, formal French style Millennium Parterre and the traditional walled garden. The walled garden contains colourful herbaceous borders, vinery & peach house, and in keeping with the tradition, the kitchen garden still supplies vegetables and soft fruit for the castle. Garden Centre, Children's Adventure Playground and a Coffee Shop specialising in homemade dishes prepared by the Duke's chef.

8 & 9 July - Gardeners' Festival.

Admission: Walled Garden (honesty box)

Castle & Grounds: Adults £6.00 Seniors/Students £5.00 Children (5 - 16) £3.25 Under 5's free
Grounds & Gardens: Adults £3.00 Seniors/Students £1.50 Children (under 16) free
Walled Garden, Garden Centre and Coffee Shop OPEN DAILY ALL YEAR
Castle - Open daily from 1 April until 29 October 2006
Enquiries 01573 223333 *www.floorscastle.com*
Donation to Scotland's Gardens Scheme

---

5. MONTEVIOT, Jedburgh & (partially)

Monteviot garden lies along a steep rise above the Teviot valley, a setting which adds a sense of drama to its many outstanding features. From the box-hedged herb garden walk in front of the House with its unique and breathtaking view of the river below, down through the sheltered terraced rose-garden, into the River Garden originally designed in the 1960s by Percy Cane. Italianate in inspiration this garden slopes down between curved borders of herbaceous plants, shrubs, and roses to a broad stone landing stage. In the Water Garden, with its three islands linked by elegant curved wooden bridges, there is an interesting variety of bog and damp-loving plants with bamboo adding a sense of mystery. Turn off A68, 3 miles north of Jedburgh B6400.

Admission £2.50 Children under 16 free

OPEN DAILY 1 April – 31 OCTOBER 12 noon – 5pm

Donation to Scotland's Gardens Scheme

---

6. ST. BOSWELLS VILLAGE AND SCARECROWS

St Boswells lies beside the Tweed in the heart of the Scottish Borders. Much of the charm of the village in summer depends upon the variety, interest and contrast of its many private gardens, all witnessing to the skill and imagination of their owners. Parking on St Boswells Village Green only where tickets and guides will be available. Teas in the Church Hall. Plant stall. Children's scarecrow competition on the Village Green.
Admission £3.00 which includes all open gardens. Children free
SUNDAY 30 JULY 2 - 6pm
40% to St Boswells Parish Church 60% net to SGS Charities

7. STABLE HOUSE, St Boswells

(Lt Col & Mrs MD Blacklock)
"A plant lovers garden" Here, in an informal design, unusual plants are combined with old fashioned roses, shrubs and herbacious plants to give all the year round interest. All in half an acre, also a courtyard garden with tender climber sand, small decorative organic vegetable garden. Teas. Plant stall. Route: two minutes from A68 on the A699 to Kelso.
JOINT OPENING WITH BENRIG & BENRIG COTTAGE, situated on the same road.
Admission £3.00 for all 3 gardens. Children free.
SUNDAY 2 JULY 2 - 6pm
40% to Mertoun & Maxton Church Fund 60% net to SGS Charities

8. WEST LEAS, Bonchester Bridge ♿ (partly)

(Mr and Mrs Robert Laidlaw)
The visitor to West Leas can share in the exciting and dramatic project on a grand scale still in the making. At its core is a passion for plants allied to a love and understanding of the land in which they are set. Collections of perennials and shrubs, many in temporary holding quarters, lighten up the landscape to magical effect. New landscaped water features, bog garden and extensive new shrub planting. A recently planted orchard, with underplantings of spring bulbs, demonstrates that the productive garden can be highly ornamental. Teas. Plant Stall.
Admission: £3.00   Children free
SUNDAY 23 JULY 2 - 6pm
40% to MacMillan Cancer Relief, Border Appeal 60% net to SGS Charities

9. YETHOLM VILLAGE

Situated at the north end of the Pennine Way and lying close to the Bowmont Water in the dramatic setting of the foothills of the Cheviots, the village of Town Yetholm offers visitors the chance to walk through several delightful gardens planted in a variety of styles and reflecting many distinctive horticultural interests. From newly established, developing and secret gardens to old and established gardens there is something here to interest everyone. The short walking distance between the gardens provides the added advantage of being able to enjoy the magnificence of the surrounding landscape to include 'Stacrough' and 'The Curr' which straddles both the Bowmont and Halterburn Valleys where evidence of ancient settlements remain. Tickets will be sold on the Village Green where there will be a produce stall to include plants, vegetables, jams and home baking.   In adition at Almond Cottage a craft stall will offer examples of local wood turning, sketches and greeting cards.   Home baked teas will also be served in the Youth Hall. Ample parking. Route: South of Kelso take the B6352 to Town Yetholm.
Admission £3.00, includes all gardens Children under 10 Free
SUNDAY 6 AUGUST 2 - 6pm
40% to RDA Borders   60% net to SGS Charities

STEWARTRY OF KIRKCUDBRIGHT

District Organiser: **Mrs C Cathcart,** Culraven, Borgue, Kirkcudbright DG6 4SG

Area Organisers: **Mrs P Addison,** Killeron Farm, Gatehouse of Fleet,
    Castle Douglas DG7 2BS

    Mrs W N Dickson, Chipperkyle, Kirkpatrick Durham, Castle Douglas DG7 3EY

    Mrs M R C Gillespie, Danevale Park, Crossmichael, Castle Douglas DG7 2LP

    Mrs W B Kirkpatrick, Rough Hills, Sandyhills, Dumfries DG5 4NZ

    Mrs B Marshall, Cairnview, Carsphairn DG7 3TQ

    Mrs J F Mayne, Hazelfield House, Auchencairn, Castle Douglas DG7 1RF

    Mrs W J McCulloch, Ardwall, Gatehouse of Fleet DG7 2EN

    Mrs M McIlvenna, Brae Neuk, Balmaclellan, Castle Douglas DG7 3QS

    Mrs S Purdie, The Old Kirk, Hardgate, Castle Douglas DG7 3LD

    Mrs C V Scott, 14 Castle Street, Kircudbright DG6 4JA

Hon. Treasurer: **Mr P Phillips,** The Old Manse, Old Ferry Road, Crossmichael
    Castle Douglas DG7 3AT

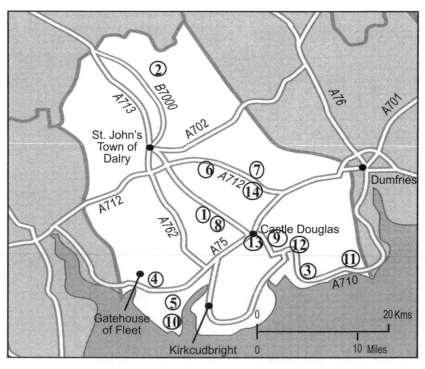

DATES OF OPENING

19 Rhonepark Crescent, Crossmichael .... May - June by appointment
Arndarroch Cottage, St John's Town of Dalry .... July - September by appointment
Barnhourie Mill, Colvend .... May - Oct by appointment
Carleton Croft, Borgue .... July to August by appointment
Corsock House, Castle Douglas   Apr - June by appointment (and for
                                                  Autumn Colours)
Danevale Park, Crossmichael .... By appointment till 1 June
Southwick House, Dumfries .... Mon 26 - Fri 30 June

Danevale Park, Crossmichael (Snowdrops).............	To be announced	
Senwick House, Borgue	Sunday 9 April	2 - 5pm
Walton Park, Castle Douglas	Sunday 30 April	2 - 5pm
Danevale Park, Crossmichael (Bluebells)	Sunday 14 May	2 - 5pm
Corsock House, Castle Douglas	Sunday 28 May	2 - 5pm
Cally Gardens, Gatehouse of Fleet	Sunday 4 June	10am - 5.30pm
Southwick House, Dumfries	Sunday 25 June	2 - 5pm
Threave Garden, Castle Douglas.............................	Sunday 9 July	9.30am - 5.30pm
Millhouse, Rhonehouse	Sunday 23 July	2 - 5pm
The Mill House, Gelston	Sunday 23 July	2 - 5pm
Arndarroch Cottage, St John's Town of Dalry	Sunday 30 July	2 - 5pm
Cally Gardens, Gatehouse of Fleet	Sunday 13 August	10am - 5.30pm
Crofts, Kirkpatrick Durham	Sunday 20 August	2 - 5pm
Arndarroch Cottage, St John's Town of Dalry	Sat & Sun 9 & 10 September	2 - 5pm

1. 19 RHONEPARK CRESCENT, Crossmichael

(Geoff Packard)
Quarter acre garden on a south west facing slope. Extensive rockery, herbaceous border, ornamental grasses and mature conifers on three levels. Village 3 miles north of Castle Douglas on the A713
Admission by donation. Children free.
OPEN BY APPOINTMENT MAY AND JUNE - TEL: 01556 670466
40% to Abbeyfield Stewartry Society Ltd (Bothwell House) 60% net to SGS Charities

2. ARNDARROCH COTTAGE, St John's Town of Dalry   ♿ (partly)

(Annikki and Matt Lindsay)
A young 2¼ acre garden created since 1991 on a windswept hillside overlooking Kendoon Loch. A great variety of trees, some species roses and shrubs have been underplanted with herbaceous plants. Small pond and bog garden. Small kitchen garden. Collections of oriental and medicinal plants. Also a collection of over 20 different bamboos. A small woodland was planted in 2000. The aim has been to create a semi-natural, wildlife friendly environment. Dogs on leads are welcome. Route: about 5 miles from St John's Town of Dalry or Carsphairn on the B7000. Follow signs to the Youth Hostel. Parking at the Cottage.
Admission £3.00 Children Free
SUNDAY 30 JULY 2 - 5pm Teas and Plant Stall. Garden quiz for children with small prizes.
SATURDAY 9 & SUNDAY 10 SEPTEMBER 2 - 5pm Plant Stall.
Also open by appointment July to September Tel: 01644 460640
40% to Dumfries & Galloway Canine Rescue Centre   60% net to SGS Charities

3. BARNHOURIE MILL, Colvend   ♿ (partly)
(Dr M R Paton)
Flowering shrubs and trees, dwarf conifers and an especially fine collection of rhododendron species. Cars free. Dalbeattie 5 miles. Route A710 from Dumfries.
Admission £3.00 Children free
MAY - OCTOBER by appointment for groups and individuals. Tel: 01387 780269
40% to Scottish Wildlife Trust 60% net to SGS Charities

---

4. CALLY GARDENS, Gatehouse of Fleet ♿
(Mr Michael Wickenden)
A specialist nursery in a fine 2.7 acre, 18th century walled garden with old vinery and bothy, all surrounded by the Cally Oak woods. Our collection of 3,500 varieties can be seen and a selection will be available pot-grown, especially rare herbaceous perennials. Forestry nature trails nearby. Route: From Dumfries take the Gatehouse turning off A75 and turn left, through the Cally Palace Hotel Gateway from where the gardens are well signposted. Admission charge: £2.50. Open Easter Saturday – last Sunday in September: Tues–Frid 2–5.30pm, Sat & Sun 10am–5.30pm. Closed Mondays.
SUNDAYS 4 JUNE & 13 AUGUST 10am - 5.30pm
40% to Save the Children Fund 60% net to SGS Charities

---

5. CARLETON CROFT, Borgue   ♿
(Mr and Mrs D J Hartley)
Cottage garden with well stocked and interesting herbaceous beds, shrubs, trees, tubs and baskets. Created for wildlife and the pleasure of gardening. On the B272 between Borgue and Gatehouse of Fleet. Teas and plant stall.
Admission by donation
OPEN BY APPOINTMENT JULY AND AUGUST Tel: 01557 870 447
40% to Wigtownshire Animal Welfare Association 60% net to SGS Charities

---

6. CORSOCK HOUSE, Castle Douglas
(Mr & Mrs M L Ingall)
Rhododendrons, woodland walks with temples, water gardens and loch. David Bryce turretted "Scottish Baronial" house in background. A limited selection of plants for sale. Teas. Cars free. Dumfries 14 miles, Castle Douglas 10 miles, Corsock half mile on A712.
Admission £3.00 Children Free
SUNDAY 28 MAY 2 - 5pm
Also open by appointment April to June and for autumn colours. Tel. 01644 440250
40% to Corsock & Kirkpatrick Durham Kirk 60% net to SGS Charities

---

7. CROFTS, Kirkpatrick Durham ♿ (partly)
(Mr & Mrs Andrew Dalton)
Victorian garden in the process of renovation and extension. Teas. Plant stall. A75 to Crocketford, then 3 miles on A712.
Admission £3.00 Children Free.
SUNDAY 20 AUGUST 2 - 5pm
40% to Corsock & Kirkpatrick Durham Church 60% net to SGS Charities

8. DANEVALE PARK, Crossmichael

(Mrs M R C Gillespie)
Open for snowdrops. Mature garden with woodland walks alongside the River Dee. Walled garden. Tea in house. Route: A713. Crossmichael 1 mile, Castle Douglas 2 miles.
Admission £2.50 Children Free
DATE for Snowdrops - TO BE ANNOUNCED
SUNDAY 14 MAY for Bluebells
Also open by appointment till 1 June Tel: 01556 670223
40% to Crossmichael Village Hall 60% net to SGS Charities (Snowdrop Opening)
40% to Edinburgh Erskine Home 60% net to SGS Charities (Bluebells Opening)

---

9. MILLHOUSE, Rhonehouse

(Bill Hean)
Small garden. mainly herbaceous and alpines. Vegetable garden. Signs in village of Rhonehouse, just off A75 west of Castle Douglas.
Admission £3.00 Children Free
JOINT OPENING WITH THE MILL HOUSE GELSTON
SUNDAY 23 JULY 2 - 5pm
40% to Buittle & Kelton Church 60% net to SGS Charities

---

10. SENWICK HOUSE, Brighouse Bay &

(Mrs Geraldine Austin)
Georgian country house set in 10 acres of mature gardens with splendid views of Brighouse Bay. Magnificent daffodil display with over 300 different varieties. Gardens feature mature trees, conifers, shrubs and woodland. Route: from Kirkcudbright take the B727 to Borgue and follow signs to Brighouse Bay. Cream teas.
Admission £3.00 Children Free
SUNDAY 9 APRIL 2 - 5pm
40% to Chest, Heart and Stroke Scotland 60% net to SGS Charities

---

11. SOUTHWICK HOUSE, Southwick &

(Mr & Mrs R H L Thomas)
Traditional formal walled garden with lily ponds, herbaceous borders, shrubs, vegetables, fruit and greenhouses. Fine trees and lawns through which flows the Southwick burn. New developments in water garden. Teas. On A710 near Caulkerbush. Dalbeattie 7 miles, Dumfries 17 miles.
Admission £3.00 Children free
SUNDAY 25 JUNE 2 - 5pm
ALSO OPEN MONDAY 26 JUNE - FRIDAY 30 JUNE - Honesty Box
20% to Perennial (GRBS) 20% to Loch Arthur 60% net to SGS Charities

---

12. THE MILL HOUSE, Gelston

(Magnus Ramsay)
A collection of plants for small gardens. Route: Entrance to village of Gelston from Castle Douglas at the 30 mile speed limit sign on B727.
Admission £3.00 Children Free
JOINT OPENING WITH MILLHOUSE RHONEHOUSE
SUNDAY 9 JULY 2 - 5pm
40% to Afghan Schools Trust 60% net to SGS Charities

13. THREAVE GARDEN, Castle Douglas ♿

(The National Trust for Scotland)
Home of the Trust's School of Practical Gardening. Spectacular daffodils in spring, colourful herbaceous borders in summer, striking autumn trees and heather garden. Plant centre. Route: A75, one mile west of Castle Douglas.
Admission £6.00 Children & OAPs £4.75 Family £14.50
SUNDAY 9 JULY 9.30am - 5.30pm
40% to The Gardens Fund of The National Trust for Scotland 60% net to SGS Charities

---

14. WALTON PARK, Castle Douglas

(Mr Jeremy Brown)
Walled garden, gentian border. Flowering shrubs, rhododendrons and azaleas. Cars free. Teas. Plant stall. Route: B794 to Corsock, 3½ miles from A75.
Admission £3.00 Children Free
SUNDAY 30 APRIL 2 - 5pm
40% to Corsock & Kirkpatrick Durham Church 60% net to SGS Charities

---

STIRLING

Joint District Organisers:	**Maud Crawford**, St Blane's House, Dunblane FK15 OER
	Lesley Stein, Southwood, Southfield Crescent, Stirling FK8 2JQ
Area Organisers:	**Carola Campbell**, Kilbryde Castle, Doune FK15 3HN
	Jean Gore, Braehead, 69 Main Street, Doune FK16 8BW
	Jane Hutchison, Settie, Kippen FK8 3HN
	Fleur McIntosh, 8 Albert Place, Stirling FK8 2QL
	Sue Stirling-Aird, Old Kippenross, Dunblane FK15 OCQ
	Helen Younger, Old Leckie, Gargunnock FK8 3BN
Hon. Treasurer	**John McIntyre**, 18 Scott Brae, Kippen FK8 3DL

DATES OF OPENING

14 Glebe Crescent, Tillicoultry .... By appointment
Arndean, By Dollar .... By appointment mid May - end June
Blairuskin Lodge, Kinlochard, by Aberfoyle .... By appointment May & June
Callander Lodge, Callander .... By appointment April - end August
Camallt, Fintry .... By appointment
Culbuie, Buchlyvie .... May - October Tuesdays 1 - 5pm
.... or by appointment
Daldrishaig House, Aberfoyle .... By appointment April, May, June & July
Gargunnock House, Gargunnock .... Wednesday's mid April - mid June
.... and by appointment
Kilbryde Castle, Dunblane` .... By appointment
The Cottage, Buchlyvie... By appointment weekdays May & June

120

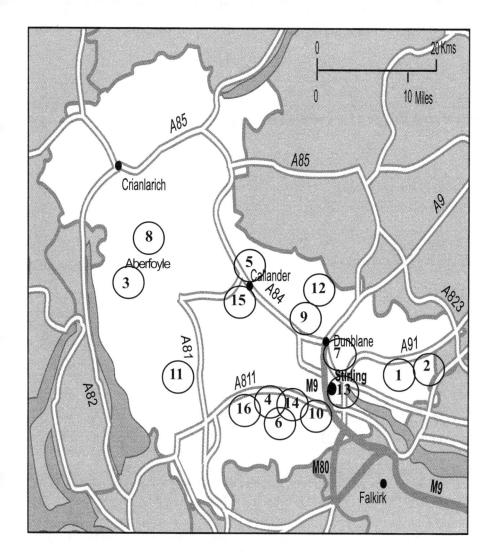

1. 14 GLEBE CRESCENT, Tillicoultry ♿

(Jim & Joy McCorgray)

Half acre beautifully designed plantsman's garden with specialist areas. Japanese, ornamental grasses, bonsai, conifer and perfumed gardens. Koi carp pool. Woodland area in spring offers paticular interest. As featured on 'The Beechgrove Garden' and in 'Gorgeous Gardens ' and 'Garden Answers' magazines. Home made teas. Good selection of home grown plants for sale. Route: A91 St Andrews/Stirling road; east end of Tillicoultry; yellow arrow at Glebe Crescent. Admission £2.50 Senior Citizens £1.50 Children Free

SUNDAY 2 JULY 1 - 5pm

Also by appointment. Tel: 01259 750484

40% to The New Struan School for Autism Appeal 60% net to SGS Charities

---

2. ARNDEAN, by Dollar

(Sir Robert & Lady Stewart)

Flowering shrubs, rhododendrons, azaleas, woodland walk. Route off A977 and A99 Admission Adults £3.00

OPEN BY APPOINTMENT MID MAY - END JUNE TEL: 01259 742527

40% to Strathcarron Hospice 60% net to SGS Charities

---

3. BLAIRUSKIN LODGE, Kinlochard, Aberfoyle

(Mr & Mrs D Miller)

Flowering shrubs, rhododendrons, woodland walk, vegetable garden, cottage garden. Route: A81 Glasgow/Aberfoyle; 6 miles from Aberfoyle on Inversnaid Road, one mile from Forest Hills. Admission £2.50 Children under 12 free

OPEN BY APPOINTMENT MAY & JUNE TEL: 01877 387249

20% to Matthew Miller Cancer Fund   20% to St Mary's Episcopal Church, Aberfoyle 60% net to SGS Charities

---

4. BRIDGE OF ALLAN GARDENS

❀ MILSEYBANK ♿   (mostly)

(Murray & Sheila Airth)

A steeply sloping garden with outstanding views, terraced for ease of access and working. Woodland garden, still being developed, with bluebells, mixed deciduous trees, rhododendrons, magnolias and camellias. Vegetable garden. A right of way to the River Allan runs alongside the property. Route: situated on the A9 between junction 11, M9 and Bridge of Allan. Milseybank is 1 mile from M9 & ¼ mile from Bridge of Allan. Lecropt Kirk is ¾ mile from M9 and ½ mile from Bridge of Allan. Milseybank is at the top of the lane at Lecropt Nursery. 250 yds from Bridge of Allan train station. Disabled parking only at house. Parking and Teas at Lecropt Kirk. Minibus service from Lecropt to Milseybank

❀ AUCHENGARROCH, Chalton Road

(Rosemary Leckie)

Small garden with herbaceous border, azaleas, rhododendrons, shrubs and trees. Teas. Route: Upper Bridge of Allan signposted from main road.

❀ GARVIA HOUSE, Fishers Green

(Garth & Sylvia Broomfield)

Half acre plantsman's garden with beach, Japanese, conifer and water gardens. Extensive rockeries with alpine plants. Home made teas. No dogs. Route: Upper Bridge of Allan signposted from main road.

122

✪ PLAKA, Pendreich Road
(Malcolm & Ann Shaw)

½ acre of semi-terraced gardens divided into outdoor rooms with wild spaces. In addition, there are rhododendrons, perennials and interesting stone features. Teas. Route from the bridge, follow Bridge of Allan Golf Club signs.

Admission Adults £2.50   Children free

SUNDAY 21 MAY 1 - 5pm

40% to Strathcarron Hospice,   60% net to SGS Charities

---

5. CALLANDER LODGE, Leny Feus, Callander
(Miss Caroline Penney)

Victorian garden laid out in 1863. Four acres of mature trees, shrubs, herbaceous and rose borders. Waterfall pool. Fern grotto. Bog garden and water garden. Woodland walk. Vegetable garden. Route: A84 west through Callander, turn right at sign for Leny Feus. Garden is at end on left.

Admission £2.50

BY APPOINTMENT APRIL - END AUGUST Tel: 01877 330 136

40% to Camphill Blair Drummond Trust   60% net to SGS Charities

---

6. CAMALLT, Fintry   ♿ (partly)
(Rebecca East and William Acton)

8 acre garden featuring some interesting daffodil cultivars dating from 1600 which carpet the woodland beside waterfalls and burn, at their best during early April. These are followed by bluebells, rhododendrons and azaleas. Herbaceous terraced borders and lawn run down to the Endrick Water. Other features include ponds and bog garden still under development. Teas in Kirk Session House 2-4. No dogs. Route: from Fintry Village B822 to Lennoxtown, approx. 1 mile then turn left to Denny on B818, Camallt entrance on right.

Admission £2.50 Children free

SUNDAY 9 APRIL 2 - 5pm Daffodil Day Bunches of daffodils for sale.

OPEN ALL YEAR BY APPOINTMENT - monitored telephone answering machine 01360 860 075

40% to The Menzies Hall Building Project 60% net to SGS Charities

---

✪ 7. CULBUIE, Buchlyvie
(Ian & Avril Galloway)

Spring collection of rhododendrons, azaleas, narcissi, bluebells, primulas and meconopsis. Woodland walk with new planting. Early summer magnolias, cornus and viburnums. Colourful perennial borders. Wild flower meadow. Good autumn colour. Lots of interest throughout this 5-acre garden with splendid views to Ben Lomond and the surrounding hills. Sorry no dogs. Route: take the A811 to Buchlyvie, turn up Culbowie Road and 'Culbuie' is almost at the top of the hill on the right.

Admission £2.50

OPEN ALL YEAR BY APPOINTMENT, TUESDAYS 1 - 5pm MAY to OCTOBER.

Please telephone 01360 850232

40% to Preshal Trust 60% net to SGS Charities

---

8. DALDRISHAIG HOUSE, Aberfoyle
(John & Fiona Blanche)

A fascinating garden in a spectacular setting on the banks of Loch Ard. Formal front garden, also rock, gravel and bog gardens, even a cliff. New raised vegetable beds (ever so small) from where more rhododendrons have been cleared. Disabled parking only.

Admission £3.00 Children free

GROUPS WELCOME BY APPOINTMENT APRIL, MAY, JUNE & JULY Tel: 01877 382223

40% to Aberfoyle Parish Church 60% net to SGS Charities

9. DUNBLANE GARDENS, Dunblane

A selection of town gardens with a large variety of interesting plants. Map/entry ticket to all gardens can be purchased at any of the open gardens. Look for the yellow "GARDEN OPEN" signs. Teas available at local cafés. Individual plant stalls. No dogs please.

Admission £3.00 OAP's £2.00 Children free

SUNDAY 11 JUNE 2 - 5pm

40% to Strathcarron Hospice 60% net to SGS Charities

10. GARGUNNOCK HOUSE, Gargunnock ♿
(Gargunnock Trustees)

Five acres of mature rhododendrons, azaleas, unusual flowering shrubs and wonderful trees with glorious autumn colour. Good plant sale all year. Dogs on lead please. Route: 5 miles west of Stirling on A811.

Admission Adults £2.50 Children free

SUNDAY 15 OCTOBER 2 - 5pm - Autumn opening and END OF SEASON PLANT SALE including rhododendrons.

AND WEDNESDAYS FROM MID APRIL - MID JUNE & IN SEPT & OCT 2 - 5pm

Also By Appointment Tel: 01786 860392

40% to Childrens Hospice Association (Scotland)   60% net to SGS Charities

❀ 11. GARTMORE VILLAGE ♿ (partly)

Several attractive and interesting small gardens in beautiful peaceful village with splendid views. Map/entry ticket to all gardens can be purchased at any of the open gardens. Look for the yellow "GARDEN OPEN" signs. Teas in village hall. Plant stall. Route: Gartmore is on a small loop road off the A81 Glasgow-Aberfoyle Road, well signposted. It is about 4 miles from Aberfoyle.

Admission Adults £3.00 Children Free

SUNDAY 9 JULY 2 - 5pm

20% to Strathcarron Hospice 20% to Children's Hospice, Balloch 60% net to SGS Charities

12. KILBRYDE CASTLE, Dunblane, Perthshire ♿ (partly)
(Sir James & Lady Campbell & Jack Fletcher)

Traditional Scottish baronial house rebuilt 1877 to replace building dating from 1461. Partly mature gardens with additions and renovations since 1970. Lawns overlooking Ardoch Burn with wood and water garden. Three miles from Dunblane and Doune, off the A820 between Dunblane and Doune. On Garden Scheme days, signposted from A820. No dogs.

GARDENERS' MARKET SUNDAY 14 MAY 11am - 5pm - Admission £3.00 Children free. Refreshments and cream teas. Full range of gardeners' stalls.

SUNDAY 18 JUNE 2 - 5pm - Admission £2.50 Under 16s & OAPs £2.00. No teas.

Also by appointment. Tel: 01786 824897

20% to Leighton Library 20% to Strathcarron Hospice 60% net to SGS Charities

13. SOUTHWOOD, Southfield Crescent, Stirling &

(John & Lesley Stein)

New town garden redesigned in 1987. ¾ acre of mixed planting including herbacous borders and lavender bed. Interesting specimen trees. Plant stalls. Home baking stall. Cream Teas. Route: From city centre signed from Carlton Cinema. From south, signed from St Ninian's Road. From west & north, signed from Drummond Place.

Admission £3.00   Children free

SUNDAY 4 JUNE 2 - 5pm

40% to Strathcarron Hospice   60% net to SGS Charities

✿ **14. THE COTTAGE, Buchlyvie**

(Olive & Russell Stevenson)

1 acre stream & woodland garden on a steep hillside site. Bridge & stonework, waterfalls, rhododendrons, azaleas, primulas, meconopsis, hostas & mature trees & shrubs. Route: A811 to Buchlyve then up Culbowie Road for ¼ mile. House on left.

Admission £2.50

BY APPOINTMENT MAY & JUNE WEEKDAYS

40% to Strathcarron Hospice 60% net to SGS Charities

---

15. THE PASS HOUSE, Kilmahog, Callander & (partly)

(Dr & Mrs D Carfrae)

Well planted medium sized garden with steep banks down to swift river. Camellias, rhododendrons, azaleas, alpines and shrubs. 2 miles from Callander on A84 to Lochearnhead.

Admission £2.50 Children free

SUNDAY 30 APRIL 2 - 5pm

40% to Crossroads Care Attendant Scheme 60% net to SGS Charities

---

16. THORNTREE, Arnprior   &

(Mark & Carol Seymour)

Charming cottage garden with flower beds around courtyard. Apple walk, fern garden and Saltire garden. Lovely views from Ben Lomond to Ben Ledi. Cream teas. Plant stall. Cake stall. No dogs please. Route: A811. In Arnprior take Fintry Road, Thorntree is second on right.

Admission £2.50 Children free

SUNDAY 25 JUNE 2 - 5pm

40% to Bannockburn Group RDA 60% net to SGS Charities

Stirling Autumn Lecture
Albert Hall, Stirling
Tuesday 26th September 10.30am - 4pm

The speakers are:

Anna Pavord, Author, Broadcaster and Co-Editor of Garden Illustrated

David Howard, Head Gardener to TRH The Prince of Wales and The Duchess of Cornwall.

Tom Hart Dyke, modern day plant hunter (kidnapped) and creator of 'The World Garden' in Kent.

Morning coffee, sandwich lunch and wine. Stalls.

Please apply for tickets, price £40, to:

Lady Edmonstone, Duntreath Castle, Blanefield, Glasgow G63 9AJ Tel: 01360 770215

40% to The Sandpiper Trust 60% net to SGS Charities

TWEEDDALE

District Organiser:	**Mrs Tricia Kennedy,** Newhall, Carlops EH26 9LY
	Mrs Georgina Seymour, Stobo Home Farm., Peebles EH45 8NX
Area Organisers:	**Mrs D Balfour-Scott,** Dreva Craig, Broughton, Biggar ML12 6HH
	Mr K St. C Cunningham, Hallmanor, Peebles EH45 9JN
	Mrs H B Marshall, Baddinsgill, West Linton, EH46 7HL
Hon. Treasurer:	**Mr Julian Birchall,** Drumelzier Old Manse, Biggar ML12 6JD

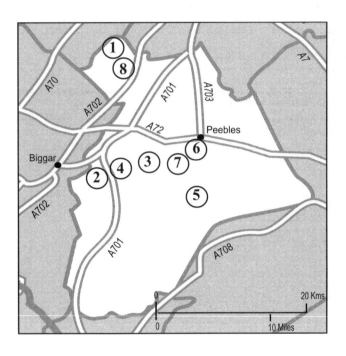

DATES OF OPENING

Baddingsgill, West Linton	Sunday 21 May	2 - 5pm
Haystoun, Peebles	Sunday 28 May	1.30 - 5.30pm
Hallmanor, Peebles..	Sunday 4 June	2 - 5.30pm
Broughton Place Stable Cottages, Broughton	Sunday 11 June	2 - 5pm
Stobo Water Garden, Stobo, Peebles	Sunday 11 June	2-5pm
West Linton Village Gardens.	Sunday 25 June	2 - 5pm
Drumelzier Old Manse, Broughton	Sunday 2 July	2 - 5pm
Broughton Place Stable Cottages, Broughton	Sunday 3 September	10am - 6pm
Dawyck Botanic Garden, Stobo	Sunday 3 September	10am - 6pm

1. BADDINSGILL, West Linton ♿ (limited access)
(Gavin and Elaine Marshall)
Beautiful woodland garden 1,000 ft up in the Pentland Hills above West Linton. Stunning situation. Woodland and riverside walks. Bluebells, azaleas and rhododendrons. Water garden. Teas and plant stall. Route: A702 to West Linton uphill past golf course.
Admission £2.50 Children Free
SUNDAY 21 MAY 2 - 5pm
40% to Multiple Sclerosis Society Scotland   60% net to SGS Charities

---

2. BROUGHTON PLACE STABLE COTTAGES, Broughton ♿ (very limited)
(David Binns and Liz Hanson)
Small garden at 800ft above sea level created from a field site since 1995 by David and Liz and packed with a most wonderful selection of plants both interesting and unusual. Well known favourites e.g. meconopsis sheldonii, Primulas, Rogersias, Cyanthus lobatus, a Thyme scree, a blue and white garden and probably the only dwarf grand fir in the country plus some unusual Scottish natives e.g. a form of Salix endemic to St. Kilda. A 4,500 year old bog root sculpture amongst others. Plant stall. Teas available locally. Route: Off A701 turn uphill towards Broughton Place at north end of Broughton.
Admission £2.50 Children Free
SUNDAY 11 JUNE 2 - 5pm
SUNDAY 3 SEPTEMBER 10am - 6pm
40% to SSPCA 60% net to SGS Charities

---

3. DAWYCK BOTANIC GARDEN, Stobo ♿ (limited access)
(Regional Garden of the Royal Botanic Garden Edinburgh and one of the National Botanic Gardens of Scotland)
Stunning collection of rare trees and shrubs. With over 300 years of tree planting Dawyck is a world famous arboretum with mature specimens of Chinese conifers, Japanese maples, Brewer's spruce, the unique Dawyck Beech and Sequoiadendrons from North America which are over 45 metres tall. Bold herbaceous plantings run along the burn. Range of trails and walks. Conservatory shop with plant sales, coffees and teas. Guide dogs only. Route: 8 miles south west of Peebles on B712.
Admission £3.50 Concessions £3.00 Children £1.00 Families £8.00
SUNDAY 3 SEPTEMBER 10am - 6pm   Guided walk 2pm.
Donation to Scotland's Gardens Scheme

---

4. DRUMELZIER OLD MANSE, Broughton ♿ (partially)
(Mr & Mrs Julian Birchall)
An old walled manse garden; herbaceous border, mixed borders and rockery. A lower shrub garden being developed down to the burn. Beautiful setting and surrounding walks. Teas. Plant stall. Signposted on B712, 10 miles south west of Peebles, 2½ miles east of Broughton.
Admission £2.50 Children free
SUNDAY 2 JULY 2 - 5pm
40% to British Red Cross Society   60% net to SGS Charities

---

5. HALLMANOR, Kirkton Manor, Peebles ⅙ (partially)
(Mr & Mrs K St C Cunningham)
Rhododendrons and azaleas, primulas, wooded grounds with loch and salmon ladder. Set in one of the most beautiful valleys in the Borders. Teas. Plant stall. Peebles 6 miles. Off A72 Peebles/Glasgow road. Follow SGS signs.
Admission £2.50 Children free
SUNDAY 4 JUNE 2 - 5.30pm
40% to Manor & Lyne Church 60% net to SGS Charities

---

6. HAYSTOUN, Peebles ⅙ (partly)
(Mr & Mrs D Coltman)
15th century house (not open). Walled garden with herbaceous beds. Wild burnside garden, created since 1980, with azaleas, rhododendrons and primulas leading to ornamental loch with beautiful views up Glensax valley. Teas. Plant stall. Dogs on lead only please. A703 Edinburgh/Peebles over Tweed bridge in Peebles, follow SGS signs for 1½ miles.
Admission £3.00 Children free
SUNDAY 28 MAY 1.30 - 5.30pm
40% to Manor & Lyne Church 60% net to SGS Charities

---

7. STOBO WATER GARDEN, Stobo, Peebles
(Mr & Mrs Hugh Seymour)
Water garden, lakes, azaleas and rhododendrons. Woodland walks. Teas locally. Dogs on a lead please. Peebles 7 miles, signposted on B712 Lyne/Broughton Road.
Admission £3.00 Children free.
SUNDAY 11 JUNE 2 - 5pm
40% to East Gate Theatre, Peebles 60% net to SGS Charities

---

8. WEST LINTON VILLAGE GARDENS ⅙ (partially)
A group of village gardens: cottage style, plantsman's and a secret courtyard showing early summer flowers, hostas, candelabra, primulas, trilliums, irises, delphiniums, lupins, aqualegias. Many more hardy perennials, shrubs and conifers. Route: A701 or A702 and follow signs. Tickets, maps, teas and plant stall in New Church Hall in the centre of the village.
Admission £3.50 includes all gardens. Children free
SUNDAY 25 JUNE 2 - 5pm
20% to Ben Walton Trust 20% to Breast Cancer Fund, Borders General Hospital 60% net to SGS Charities

---

WIGTOWN

District Organiser: **Mrs Francis Brewis,** Ardwell House, Stranraer DG9 9LY

Area Organisers: **Mrs V Wolseley Brinton,** Chlenry, Castle Kennedy,
Stranraer DG9 8SL
Mrs Andrew Gladstone, Craichlaw, Kirkcowan,
Newton Stewart DG8 0DQ

Hon. Treasurer: **Mr G Fleming,** Ardgour, Stoneykirk, Stranraer DG9 9DL

128

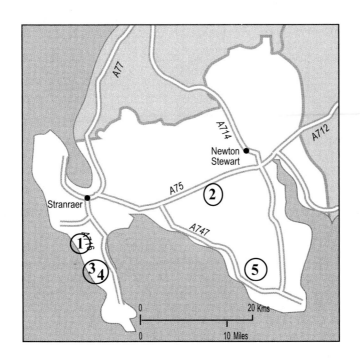

DATES OF OPENING

Ardwell House Gardens, Ardwell .... Daily 1 April - 30 September   10am - 5pm
Logan House Gardens, Port Logan .... Daily 1 February - 1 April   10am - 4pm
.... 2 April - 31 August   9am - 6pm

Logan House Gardens, Port Logan .... Sunday 7 May   9am - 6pm
Woodfall Gardens, Glasserton .... Sunday 14 May   2 - 5.30pm
Logan Botanic Garden, Port Logan .... Sunday 28 May   10am - 6pm
Craichlaw, Kirkcowan .... Sunday 2 July   2 - 5pm
Woodfall Gardens, Glasserton .... Sunday 9 July   2 - 5pm

1. ARDWELL HOUSE GARDENS, Ardwell, Stranraer

(Mr & Mrs Francis Brewis)
Daffodils, spring flowers, rhododendrons, flowering shrubs, coloured foliage and rock plants.
Moist garden at smaller pond and a walk round larger ponds, with views over Luce Bay. Plants
for sale and self-pick fruit in season. Collecting box. House not open. Dogs welcome on leads.
Picnic site on shore. Stranraer 10 miles. Route A76 towards Mull of Galloway.
Admission £3.00 Concessions £2.00 Children under 14 free
DAILY 1 APRIL - 30 SEPTEMBER 10am - 5pm
Donation to Scotland's Gardens Scheme

2. CRAICHLAW, Kirkcowan   ♿

(Mr & Mrs Andrew Gladstone)

Formal garden around the house, with herbaceous borders. Set in extensive grounds with lawns, lochs and woodland. A path around the main loch leads to a water garden returning past an orchard of old Scottish apple varieties. Teas. Plant stall. Signposted off A75, 8 miles west of Newton Stewart and B733, one mile west of Kirkcowan.

Admission £2.50 Accompanied children under 14 free

SUNDAY 2 JULY 2 - 5pm

40% to Kirkcowan Parish Church   60% net to SGS Charities

---

3. LOGAN BOTANIC GARDEN, Port Logan, by Stranraer   ♿

(Regional Garden of the Royal Botanic Garden Edinburgh and one of the National Botanic Gardens of Scotland)

At the south-western tip of Scotland lies, Logan unrivalled as the county's most exotic garden. With a mild climate washed by the Gulf Stream, a remarkable collection of bizarre and beautiful plants, especially from the southern hemisphere, flourish out-of-doors. Enjoy the colourful walled garden with its magnificent tree ferns, palms and borders and the contrasting woodland garden with its unworldly gunnera bog. Explore the Discovery Centre or take an audio tour. Home baking and Botanics Shop. Guide dogs only. Route: 10 miles south of Stranraer on A716, then 2½ miles from Ardwell village.

Admission : £3.50 Concessions £3.00 Children £1.00 Family £8.00

SUNDAY 28 MAY 10am - 6pm

40% to Royal Botanic Garden Edinburgh   60% net to SGS Charities

---

4. LOGAN HOUSE GARDENS, Port Logan, by Stranraer   ♿

(Mr & Mrs Roberts)

Queen Anne house, 1701. Rare exotic tropical plants and shrubs. Fine specie and hybrid rhododendrons. Route: 14 miles south of Stranraer on A716, 2½ miles from Ardwell village.

Admission: £2.00 Children under 16 Free

SUNDAY 7 MAY 9am -6pm

Also open daily: 1 February - 1 April 10am - 4pm   2 April- 31 August   9am - 6pm

40% to Port Logan Hall Fund   60% net to SGS Charities

---

5. WOODFALL GARDENS, Glasserton   ♿

(David and Lesley Roberts)

A 3 acre, 18th Century walled garden undergoing revitalisation. As well as the remains of the original garden buildings there are mixed borders, a woodland area, a parterre and a productive potager. For the July opening, The Swallow Theatre will provide an entertainment at 4pm (weather permitting). Plant stall. Sorry no dogs. 2 miles south of Whithorn by junction off A746/747

Admission Adults £2.50 Concessions £2.00 Accompanied children under 14 free

SUNDAY 14 MAY & 9 JULY 2 - 5.30pm

May Opening - 30% to the Swallow Theatre   10% to Glasserton and Isle of Whithorn Church 60% net to SGS Charities

July Opening - 30% Alzheimers (Scotland) 10% to Glasserton and Isle of Whithorn Church 60% net to SGS Charities

---

THE SCOTTISH ROCK GARDEN CLUB

ngs gardens open for charity

The National Gardens Scheme (NGS)

- Over 3,500 gardens, mostly private, open for the NGS every year
- The NGS donates nearly £2 million annually to nursing, caring and gardening charities
- Three quarters of a million people visit NGS gardens in England and Wales every year
- The Yellow Book, listing all NGS gardens, is the UK's most popular garden visiting guide.

The National Gardens Scheme Hatchlands Park, East Clandon, Surrey GU4 7RT
Tel 01483 211535 **Fax** 01483 211537 **Email** ngs@ngs.org.uk **Web** www.ngs.org.uk

Registered Charity No. 279284

AUSTRALIA'S OPEN GARDEN SCHEME

A ROUND 700 inspiring private gardens drawn from every Australian state and territory feature in our annual program.

Included are tropical gardens in the Northern Territory and Queensland, awe-inspiring arid zone gardens, traditional gardens in the temperate south, gardens which feature Australia's unique flora, and gardens designed by many of Australia's contemporary designers.

Our full colour guidebook is published each August by ABC Books and every entry includes a full description, map references and directions, opening details and amenities.

State-by-state calendars make it easy to plan a personal itinerary, and a special index identifies gardens with a particular plant collection or area of interest.

Also included are exhaustive listings of regularly open gardens around the country, as well as some of the many gardens which offer accommodation.

PRESIDENT: *Mrs Malcolm Fraser*
CHIEF EXECUTIVE OFFICER: *Neil Robertson*
Westport, New Gisborne, Victoria 3438
Tel +61 3 5428 4557
Fax +61 3 5428 4558
email: national@opengarden.org.au
website: www.opengarden.org.au
Australia's Open Garden Scheme ABN 60 057 467 553

ABC
BOOKS

"IndependentAge brings a ray of sunshine into my life"

IndependentAge is a charity that champions independence for older people. It provides financial help and friendship to assist people to stay in their homes and we have over 70 volunteer visitors in Scotland who support our beneficiaries. If you would like more information about our work please complete the coupon.

Independent*Age*

Supporting older people at home

The Royal United Kingdom Beneficent Association
Charity Registration Number 210729

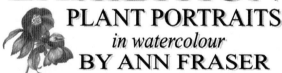
TO ADVERTISE IN THESE PAGES PLEASE CONTACT
Scotland's Gardens Scheme
22 Rutland Square
Edinburgh EH1 2BB
Tel: 0131 229 1870
Fax 0131 229 0443
email: *office@sgsgardens.fsnet.co.uk*

ANDERSON STRATHERN PRIVATE CLIENT SERVICES ARE DELIGHTED TO BE SPONSORS OF SCOTLAND'S GARDEN SCHEME HANDBOOK AND WEBSITE

Anderson Strathern Private Client Services are delighted to be involved with Scotland's Gardens Scheme and are proud to be associated with such a worthy cause. As a firm, we have acted as legal advisors to Scotland's Gardens Scheme for many years.

We have a long established reputation as a leader in the Scottish legal marketplace for services to private clients, trusts and charities.

Our aim is to become long-term partners with our clients, helping them in their wealth management planning to preserve their assets from tax and ensure that wealth is maximised and passed on according to their wishes.

This approach has helped us become successful in providing high quality independent advice and a personal service with emphasis on each client's particular needs. We have a team of experienced private client lawyers, tax and financial services specialists providing proactive and comprehensive advice.

As a firm, we also deal with all legal issues relating to residential property and rural estates. We are recognised by leading legal directories as, in particular, in the top rank in Scotland for agricultural and estates work.

Anderson Strathern, as a leading law firm, also provides a full range of advice to corporate and commercial clients. We are based in modern offices in the heart of Edinburgh with over 200 people.

If you would like to find out more about how we could you help you, please contact us on 0131 270 7700 or have a look on our website at www.andersonstrathern.co.uk.

Colin Henderson
Head of Private Client Services

1 Rutland Court, Edinburgh EH3 8EY www.andersonstrathern.co.uk

136

The National Trust
for Scotland

1931-2006

Celebrating 75 Years at the

Heart of the Nation

To join us in this special year, call 0131 243 9555
Or visit the charity's website – www.nts.org.uk

Dumfries & Galloway

Broughton House and Garden

Off A711/A755, at 12 High Street, Kirkcudbright

A fascinating 18th-century house in a delightful harbour town, this was the home and studio from 1901 to 1933 of the artist E A Hornel, one of the 'Glasgow Boys'. His studio overlooks the one-acre Japanese-style garden he designed after visits to the Far East.

OPEN: *GARDEN: 1 Feb to 31 Mar, Mon-Fri 11-4. HOUSE AND GARDEN: Good Fri to 30 Sep, Thurs-Mon, 12-5.*

Adult	Family	1 Parent	Concession
£8	£20	£16	£5

Threave

Threave

Off A75, 1m west of Castle Douglas

Best known for its spectacular daffodils, Threave is also a garden for all seasons, with bright herbaceous beds in summer, and vibrant trees and heather garden in autumn. The Victorian House, now open to visitors, is also home to the Trust's School of Practical Gardening. Visitor Centre with exhibition, shop and licensed restaurant; plant sales, guided walks.

OPEN: *ESTATE All year, daily. WALLED GARDEN AND GLASSHOUSES: all year, daily 9.30-5. VISITOR CENTRE, COUNTRYSIDE CENTRE, EXHIBITION, SHOP AND PLANT CENTRE: 1 Feb to 31 Mar and 1 Nov to 23 Dec, daily 10-4; 1 Apr to 31 Oct, daily 9.30-5.30. RESTAURANT: 1 Feb to 31 Mar and 1 Nov to 23 Dec, daily 10-4; 1 Apr to 31 Oct, daily 10-5. HOUSE: 1 Apr to 31 Oct, Wed, Thu, Fri, Sun 11-3.30.*

Adult	Family	1 Parent	Concession
£10	£25	£20	£7

Scottish Borders

Harmony Garden

In Melrose, opposite the Abbey

Wander through this tranquil garden's herbaceous borders, lawns and fruit and vegetable plots, and enjoy fine views of the Abbey and Eildon Hills.

OPEN: *Good Friday to 30 Sep, Mon-Sat 10-5, Sun 1-5.*

Adult	Family	1 Parent	Concession
£3	£8	£6	£2

Priorwood Gift Shop & Garden

In Melrose, beside the Abbey

Overlooked by the Abbey ruins, this unique garden produces plants for a superb variety of dried flower arrangements, made and sold here. The orchard contains many historic apple varieties.

OPEN: *SHOP: 6 Jan to 31 Mar, Mon-Sat 12-4; 1 Apr to 24 Dec, Mon-Sat 10-5, Sun 1-5. GARDEN: Good Fri to 24 Dec (same opening times as shop)*

Adult	Family	1 Parent	Concession
£3	£8	£6	£2

Ayrshire and Arran

Brodick Castle, Country Park and Goatfell

Isle of Arran. Ferry: Ardrossan to Brodick (55 mins) connecting bus to Reception Centre (2m). Ferry between Claonaig and Lochranza (north Arran), frequent in summer, limited in winter; tel Caledonian MacBrayne. All-inclusive travel and admission ticket from Strathclyde Passenger Transport Stations (0870) 608 2608.

Built on the site of a Viking fortress and partly dating from the 13th century, this magnificent castle overlooks Brodick Bay and has as a backdrop the majestic Goatfell mountain range. The woodland garden, specialising in rhododendrons, is one of Europe's finest, where plants from the Himalayas, Burma and China flourish. Licensed restaurant, gift shop, plant sales, guided walks.

OPEN: *CASTLE, GARDEN, AND VISITOR FACILITIES: 1 Apr to 29 Oct, daily 11-4.30 (closes 3.30 in Oct). Last admission 30 mins before closing; SHOP open 29 Oct to 24 Dec, Fri-Sun 10-3.30;*

COUNTRY PARK open all year daily.

Adult	Family	1 Parent	Concession
£10	£25	£20	£7

Culzean Castle and Country Park

12m south of Ayr, on A719, 4m west of Maybole, off A77

One of Scotland's major attractions – a perfect day out for all the family. Robert Adam's romantic 18th-century masterpiece is perched on a cliff high above the Firth of Clyde. The Fountain Garden lies in front of the castle with terraces and herbaceous borders reflecting its Georgian elegance.

The extensive country park offers beaches and rockpools, parklands, gardens, woodland walks and adventure playground. It contains fascinating restored buildings contemporary with the castle. Visitor Centre, shops, plant sales, restaurants and exhibitions. Ranger service events and guided walks.

OPEN: *CASTLE, GARDEN AND VISITOR FACILITIES: 1 Apr to 29 Oct, daily 10.30-5 (last entry 4); SHOPS AND RESTAURANTS open 29 Oct to 31 Mar, Thur-Sun 11-4; Country Park open all year, daily.*

Adult	Family	1 Parent	Concession
£12	£30	£25	£8

Greater Glasgow

Geilston Garden

On the A814 at west end of Cardross, 18m north-west of Glasgow

A delightful garden, laid out over 200 years ago, and retaining a sense of private space into which the visitor is invited. Attractive features include a walled garden and a burn, winding through the wooded glen.

OPEN: *1 Apr to 31 Oct, daily 9.30-5. House not open.*

Adult	Family	1 Parent	Concession
£5	£14	£10	£4

Greenbank Garden

Flenders Road, off Mearns Road, Clarkston. Off M77 and A726, 6m south of Glasgow city centre

A unique walled garden with plants and designs of particular interest to suburban gardeners. Fountains, woodland walk and special area for disabled visitors. Shop, plant sales, and gardening demonstrations throughout the year.

OPEN: *GARDEN: all year, daily 9.30-sunset. SHOP AND TEAROOM: Good Friday to 31 Oct, daily 11-5; 1 Nov to 31 Mar, Sat/Sun 2-4. HOUSE: Good Friday to 31 Oct, Sun 2-4.*

Adult	Family	1 Parent	Concession
£5	£14	£10	£4

Lothians and Fife

Inveresk Lodge Garden

A6124, near Musselburgh, 6m east of Edinburgh

This sunny hillside garden in the historic village of Inveresk entices visitors with its colourful herbaceous beds, attractive shrubs and old roses selected by Graham Stuart Thomas. Restored Edwardian conservatory with aviary.

OPEN: *All year, daily 10-6 or dusk if earlier.*

Adult	Family	1 Parent	Concession
£3	£8	£6	£2

Malleny Garden

Off the A70, in Balerno, 6m west of Edinburgh city centre

A peaceful walled garden with a collection of old-fashioned roses and fine herbaceous borders. Special features are the 400-year-old clipped yew trees.

OPEN: *All year, daily 10-6 or dusk if earlier.*

Adult	Family	1 Parent	Concession
£3	£8	£6	£2

Malleny Garden

Royal Burgh of Culross

Off A985, 12m west of Forth Road Bridge and 4m east of Kincardine Bridge, Fife

Relive the domestic life of the 16th and 17th centuries amid the old buildings and cobbled streets of this Royal Burgh on the River Forth. A model 17th-century garden has been recreated behind Culross Palace to show the range of plants available and includes vegetables, culinary and medicinal herbs, soft fruits and ornamental shrubs. Shop and tearoom.

OPEN: *PALACE, STUDY, TOWN HOUSE AND TEAROOM: Good Friday to 30 Sep, Thurs-Mon 12-5 Garden open all year daily, 10-6, or sunset if earlier.*

Adult	Family	1 Parent	Concession
£5	£14	£10	£4

Falkland Palace, Garden and Town Hall

A912, 11m north of Kirkcaldy. 10m from M90, junction 8

Set in a medieval village, the Royal Palace of Falkland is a superb example of Renaissance architecture. The stunning gardens were restored to a design by Percy Cane and give a long-lasting display — from spring-flowering cherry trees to the rich autumn colouring of maples. Exhibition and gift shop.

OPEN: *1 March to 31 October, Mon-Sat 10-5, Sun 1-5.*

Adult	Family	1 Parent	Concession
£8	£20	£16	£5

Hill of Tarvit Mansionhouse and Garden

Off A916, 2m south of Cupar

This fine house and garden were rebuilt in 1906 by the renowned Scottish architect Sir Robert Lorimer, for a Dundee industrialist, whose superb collection of furniture is on view. Visitors can wander through the fragrant walled garden, linger on the terraces or enjoy the heady scent of roses in the sunken garden. Shop and tearoom.

OPEN: *Good Friday to 31 May, Thurs-Mon, 1-5; 1 June to 31 Aug, daily 1-5; 1 Sept to 8 Oct, Thurs-Mon, 1-5. ESTATE open all year, daily*

Adult	Family	1 Parent	Concession
£8	£20	£16	£5

Kellie Castle and Garden

On B9171, 3m north of Pittenweem

This superb castle dates from the 14th century and was sympathetically restored by the Lorimer family in the late 19th century. The late Victorian garden has a selection of old-fashioned roses and herbaceous plants, cultivated organically. Shop and tearoom.

OPEN: *CASTLE: Good Friday to Easter Monday and 1 May to 30 Sep, daily 1-5. TEAROOM AND SHOP: same dates but opens at 12 (noon). GARDEN: all year, daily 9.30-5.30. GROUNDS: all year, daily.*

Adult	Family	1 Parent	Concession
£8	£20	£16	£5

Perthshire and Angus

Branklyn Garden

116 Dundee Road, Perth

This attractive garden was first established in 1922. It contains outstanding collections of rhododendrons, alpines, herbaceous and peat-

Azaleas at Branklyn Garden

garden plants and is particularly famed for its *Meconopsis* and its autumn colour.

OPEN:
1 Apr to 30 Oct, daily 10-5; SHOP - opening times vary throughout year.

Adult	Family	1 Parent	Concession
£5	£14	£10	£4

House of Dun

3 miles west of Montrose on the A935

This beautiful house, overlooking the Montrose Basin, was designed by William Adam in 1730. The restored walled garden displays period herbaceous and rose borders. Shop, restaurant, woodland walks.

OPEN: *HOUSE, SHOP AND RESTAURANT: Good Friday to 30 Jun and 1 to 30 Sep, Wed-Sun (closed Mon and Tue*) 12.30-5.30; 1 Jul to 31 Aug, daily 11.30-5.30. Last admission 45 mins before closing. *NB: Property will be open Bank Holidays from Fri-Mon inclusive.*

Adult	Family	1 Parent	Concession
£8	£20	£16	£5

Aberdeen and Grampian

Castle Fraser and Garden

Off A944, 4m north of Dunecht and 16m west of Aberdeen

One of the grandest Castles of Mar, this magnificent building was completed in 1636 by two master mason families. Walled garden, woodland walks, plant sales, adventure playground, courtyard café and shop.

OPEN: *CASTLE, SHOP AND TEAROOM: Good Friday to 30 Jun, daily (but closed Fri and Mon*) 12-5; 1 Jul to 31 Aug, daily 11-5; 1 to 30 Sep, daily (but closed Fri and Mon) 12-5. Last admission 45 mins before closing. SHOP also open 1 Nov to 18 Dec, Sat/Sun 12-4. *NB: Property will be open Bank Holidays from Fri-Mon inclusive.*

Adult	Family	1 Parent	Concession
£8	£20	£16	£5

Crathes Castle, Garden and Estate

On A93, 3m east of Banchory and 15m west of Aberdeen

Turrets, gargoyles and superb original painted ceilings are features of this enchanting castle, built in the late 16th century. The eight gardens within the walled garden provide a wonderful display all year round. Visitor Centre, restaurant, shop and plant sales, exciting trails and an adventure playground.

OPEN: *CASTLE AND VISITOR CENTRE: 1 Apr to 31 Aug, daily 10-5.30; 1 to 30 Sep, daily 10.30-5.30; 1 to 31 Oct, daily 10.30-4.30; 1 Nov to 31 Mar, Thursday to Sunday 10.30-3.45. PLANT SALES: same dates but weekends only in Oct and closed Nov-Mar. RESTAURANT AND SHOP: 1 Apr to 30 Sep, daily 10-5.30; 1 to 31 Oct, daily 10-4.30; 1 Nov to 31 Mar, daily 10-4.*

Adult	Family	1 Parent	Concession
£10	£25	£20	£7

Drum Castle and Garden

Off A93, 3m west of Peterculter, 8m east of Banchory and 10m west of Aberdeen

The late 13th-century keep, fine adjoining Jacobean mansion house and the additions of Victorian lairds make Drum unique. The Garden of Historic Roses represents different periods of gardening from the 17th to the 20th centuries. Woodland trails, children's playground, shop and tearoom.

OPEN: *CASTLE: Good Friday to 30 Jun, daily (but not Tues or Fri) 12.30-5; 1 Jul to 31 Aug, daily 11-5; 1 to 30 Sep, daily (but not Tues or Fri) 12.30-5. Last admission 45 mins before closing. GARDEN OF HISTORIC ROSES: Good Friday to 30 Sep, daily 11-6. GROUNDS open all year, daily.*

Adult	Family	1 Parent	Concession
£8	£20	£16	£5

Fyvie Castle

Off A947, 8m south-east of Turriff and 25m north of Aberdeen

The charm of Fyvie ranges from its 13th-century origins to its opulent Edwardian interiors.

Pitmedden Garden

Arduaine Garden

Superb collection of arms and armour and paintings, including works by Raeburn and Gainsborough. Stroll around the picturesque lake, or visit the restored 1903 racquet court and bowling alley. Shop and tearoom.

OPEN: *CASTLE: Good Friday to 30 Jun and 1 to 30 Sep, Sat-Wed (closed Thu and Fri*) 12-5; 1 Jul to 31 Aug, daily 11-5. Last admission 4.15. *NB: Property will be open Bank Holidays from Fri-Mon inclusive. GROUNDS: open all year, daily.*

Adult	Family	1 Parent	Concession
£8	£20	£16	£5

Haddo House

Off B999, near Tarves, 19m north of Aberdeen

This elegant mansion house boasts sumptuous Victorian interiors beneath a crisp Georgian exterior. Noted for fine furniture and paintings, Haddo also has a delightful terrace garden, leading to a Country Park with lakes, walks and monuments. Shop, plant sales and restaurant.

OPEN: *HOUSE: Good Friday to Easter Monday 11-4.30; May to Jun, Sat/Sun only 11-4.30; 1 Jul to 31 Aug, daily 11-4.30; Sep, Sat/Sun only 11-4.30. STABLES SHOP AND TEAROOM: Good Friday to 30 Jun, Fri-Mon 11-5; 1 Jul to 31 Aug, daily 11-5; Sep to Xmas Fayre (1st weekend in Nov), Fri-Mon 11-5. GARDEN: all year, daily.*

Adult	Family	1 Parent	Concession
£8	£20	£16	£5

Leith Hall and Garden

On B9002, 1m west of Kennethmont and 34m north-west of Aberdeen

This mansion house was the home for almost 300 years of the Leith family, and the elegantly furnished rooms reflect their lifestyle. Outside, wander among the glorious herbaceous borders or explore the estate trails. Picnic area and tearoom.

OPEN: *HALL: Easter weekend 12-5; May to June, open weekends 12-5; 1 Jul to 31 Aug, daily 12-5; September, weekends 12-5. Last ticket 4.15. GARDEN AND GROUNDS open all year, daily.*

Adult	Family	1 Parent	Concession
£8	£20	£16	£5

Pitmedden Garden

On A920, 1m west of Pitmedden village and 14m north of Aberdeen

In the Great Garden, the elaborate original parterre designs of the 17th century have been carefully re-created and are spectacularly filled in summer with some 40,000 annual flowers. Picnic area, shop, tearoom.

OPEN: *GARDEN, MUSEUM of FARMING LIFE, SHOP AND TEAROOM: 1 May to 30 Sep, daily 10-5.30. Last admission at 5. GROUNDS: all year, daily.*

Adult	Family	1 Parent	Concession
£5	£14	£10	£4

Highlands

Arduaine Garden

On A816, 20m south of Oban and 18m north of Lochgilphead

Arduaine boasts spectacular rhododendrons and azaleas in late spring and early summer, but its perennial borders are magnificent throughout the season. Stroll through the woodland to the coastal viewpoint, or relax in the water garden.

Crarae Garden   *Inverewe Garden*

OPEN: *RECEPTION CENTRE: Good Friday to 30 Sep, daily, 9.30-4.30. GARDEN: all year, daily 9.30-sunset.*

Adult	Family	1 Parent	Concession
£5	£14	£10	£4

Balmacara Estate and Lochalsh Woodland Garden

A87, 3m east of Kyle of Lochalsh

A crofting estate of 6,795 acres with superb views of Skye and Applecross. Lochalsh Woodland Garden enjoys a tranquil setting by the shore of Loch Alsh and has a collection of hardy ferns, fuchsias, hydrangeas, bamboos and rhododendrons.

OPEN: *ESTATE: all year, daily. WOODLAND GARDEN: all year, daily 9-sunset. RECEPTION KIOSK: 1 Apr to 30 Sep, daily 9-5. BALMACARA SQUARE VISITOR CENTRE: 1 Apr to 30 Sep, daily 9-5 (Fri 9-4).*

Pay and display £2

Brodie Castle

Off A96 4^{1}/$_{2}$m west of Forres and 24m east of Inverness

A 16th-century tower house with 17th- and 19th-century additions, Brodie has unusual plaster ceilings, a major art collection, porcelain and fine furniture. In springtime the grounds are carpeted with the daffodils for which the castle is rightly famous.

OPEN: *CASTLE: 10 to 30 April, daily 10.30-5; 1 May to 30 June, Sun-Thurs 10.30-5; 1 Jul to 31 Aug, daily 10.30-5; 1 to 30 Sep, Sun-Thurs 10.30-5.*

Adult	Family	1 Parent	Concession
£8	£20	£16	£5

Crarae Garden

A83, 10m south of Inveraray

Set on a hillside down which tumbles the Crarae Burn, this delightful garden is reminiscent of a Himalayan gorge. Tree and shrub collections are rich and diverse. The garden contains one of the best collections of the genus *Rhododendron* in Scotland, unusually rich in cultivars, as well as part of the National Collection of *Nothofagus* and particularly good representations of *Acer, Eucalyptus, Eucryphia* and *Sorbus*. The autumn colours of the leaves and berries are well worth a visit too. Plant sales, shop and tearoom.

OPEN: *VISITOR CENTRE: Good Friday to 30 Sep, daily 10-5. GARDEN: all year, daily 9.30-sunset.*

Adult	Family	1 Parent	Concession
£5	£14	£10	£4

Inverewe Garden

On A832, by Poolewe, 6m north-east of Gairloch

The tallest Australian gum trees in Britain, sweet-scented Chinese rhododendrons, exotic trees from Chile and Blue Nile lilies from South Africa, all grow here in this spectacular lochside setting, favoured by the warm currents of the North Atlantic Drift. Visitor Centre, shop, plant sales, licensed restaurant.

OPEN: *GARDEN: all year, daily 9.30-4; extended hours 1 April to 31 Oct, daily 9.30-9 or sunset if earlier. VISITOR CENTRE AND SHOP: 1 Apr to 30 Sep, daily 9.30-5; 1 to 31 Oct, daily 9.30-4. RESTAURANT: 1 Apr to 30 Sep, daily 10-5; 1 to 31 Oct, daily 10-4.*

Adult	Family	1 Parent	Concession
£8	£20	£16	£5

The National Trust
for Scotland

Plants for Sale!

We hope you enjoy your visit to a magical National Trust for Scotland garden.
At some of our gardens we can offer you the perfect souvenir —
a chance to recreate a bit of that garden in your own garden.
We now sell plants from 17 of our garden properties as listed below:

- **Falkland Palace**
- **Glencoe**
- **Greenbank Garden**
- **Inverewe Garden**
- **Pitmedden Garden**
- **Threave Garden**

- **Killiecrankie**
- **Hugh Miller Museum & Birthplace Cottage**
- **House of Dun**
- **Branklyn Garden**
- **Brodick Castle**

- **Castle Fraser**
- **Crathes Castle**
- **Culzean Castle**
- **Hill of Tarvit**
- **Crarae Garden**
- **Drum Castle**

This varies from a few tables of our home grown plants at some properties,
to a full blown plant centre with a wide selection of shrubs, rhododendrons,
herbaceous plants, alpines and roses at others. Some of the plants
will have been grown in the garden.

We are delighted to be able to offer plants like the famous Primula 'Inverewe'
and Crocosmia 'Culzean Pink'. We also offer a wide selection of bulbs in
season and some of the gardens now produce their own packets of seed.

The next time you visit a National Trust for Scotland property look out
for the exciting range of garden plants on offer.

All the proceeds from the sales contribute to the vital
conservation work of the Trust.

For more information please contact our properties directly.

Index to Gardens

Index to Advertisers

TO ADVERTISE IN THESE PAGES PLEASE CONTACT

Scotland's Gardens Scheme

22 Rutland Square

Edinburgh EH1 2BB

Tel: 0131 229 1870 Fax 0131 229 0443

email: *office@sgsgardens.fsnet.co.uk*

GARDENS OF SCOTLAND
2007

Order now and your copy will be posted to you on publication in February

Scotland's Gardens Scheme
22 Rutland Square
Edinburgh EH1 2BB

Please   send me_____ copy/copies of
"Gardens of Scotland 2007
Price £6.00, to include p&p, as soon as it is available
I enclose a cheque/postal order made payable to
Scotland's Gardens Scheme

Name...

Address...

Post Code...................